BLOOMSBURY CURRICULUM BASICS

Teaching Primary Computing

BLOOMSBURY CURRICULUM BASICS

Teaching Primary Computing

By Martin Burrett
@ICTmagic

B L O O M S B U R Y

LONDON · OXFORD · NEW YORK · NEW DELHI · SYDNEY

Bloomsbury Education
An imprint of Bloomsbury Publishing Plc

50 Bedford Square   1385 Broadway
London   New York
WC1B 3DP   NY 10018
UK   USA

www.bloomsbury.com

Bloomsbury is a registered trademark of Bloomsbury Publishing Plc

First published 2016

Text © Martin Burrett, 2016
Illustrations © Garry Davies, 2016
Cover illustrations © Shutterstock, 2016

British Library Cataloguing-in-Publication Data
A catalogue record for this book is available from the British Library.

ISBN:
PB 978-1-4729-2102-4
ePub 978-1-4729-2104-8
ePDF 978-1-4729-2103-1

Library of Congress Cataloging-in-Publication Data
A catalog record for this book is available from the Library of Congress.

10 9 8 7 6 5 4 3 2 1

Typeset by NewGen Knowledge Works (P) Ltd., Chennai, India
Printed and bound in Great Britain by CPI Group (UK) Ltd, Croydon CR0 4YY

This book is produced using paper that is made from wood grown in managed, sustainable
forests. It is natural, renewable and recyclable. The logging and manufacturing processes
conform to the environmental regulations of the country of origin.

To view more of our titles please visit www.bloomsbury.com

Other titles in the Bloomsbury Curriculum Basics series:

Teaching Primary History by Matthew Howorth

Teaching Primary Science by Peter Riley

Teaching Primary French by Amanda Barton and Angela McLachlan

Teaching Primary Spanish by Amanda Barton and Angela McLachlan

Table of Contents

Year 3

Year 4

Year 5

Year 6

For Xiong Fu

Thank you for your infinite patience and support,
which has made this book and many other things possible;

and

For William and James

My tech wizards and beta testers.

Introduction

About this book

The activities and ideas in this book were developed through my efforts to bring a hands-on digital dimension to the learning of the children both in my own class and the wider school. Every activity has been tried with my pupils over the years, and it is my hope that they will be a welcome resource for teachers who are just beginning their digital learning journey, whilst at the same time offering exciting ideas for experienced practitioners who are already well-versed in the ways of digital education. As is repeated time and again in this book, remixing ideas is the beginning of improvement and innovation, so tailor the lessons to meet the learning needs of your pupils, in your class.

Computing is unlike most other subject as the basic tools are different in each school. Every school has its own ecosystem of computers, devices, operating systems, policies and network restrictions, and budgets. For this reason, I have mostly used free tools, which operate across many platforms – or at least the common devices and systems that I have encountered in primary schools. I have provided alternative platforms for educators to expand if they have the tools and resources to do so but I have designed this book so that the vast majority of activities are accessible to the maximum number of teachers and pupils.

This book has been based on the English National Curriculum but there are many similarities between this and the other curricula in other parts of the UK and beyond. Despite this book being organised by year group, it is better to think of these as years of study. The activities build on prior skills found in earlier sections, so if you are updating your computing curriculum and teaching in the latter years of primary, you need to be aware that the pupils may need skills covered earlier in the resource to access the later material.

Like any subject, the tendrils of computing intertwine and overlap with other areas of the curriculum, and this book reflects the cross-curricular nature of primary school learning by offering further ideas to enhance other subject areas or to offer stimuli for the pupils' computing projects. Where possible, adapt the activities in this book to encompass topics and ideas from the wider curriculum.

Covering the National Curriculum

There are many aspects to the computing National Curriculum for England. The various strands can be grouped into three main areas, each of which is covered in every year of study throughout this book:

Using and understanding computing

Digital technology is entwined with every aspect of the modern world. We use it to work, play and learn. We are even beginning to wear it, using Smart technology in clothing and accessories. The National Curriculum is a little vague on what to focus on in class though, especially at KS1. In this book I will explore how pupils can create and interact with various types of media, information systems, devices and uses for digital technology, drawing upon my own experience as a classroom teacher.

e-Savvy

Knowing how to use digital technology is only half of the story. There are so many ways to get online and connect with people from around the world. This has brought about a revolution in the way we work, communicate and interact. However, this ever-closer interconnectedness has its challenges, especially for those unaware of the potential problems. As well as learning about the very real dangers and knowing how to stay safe online with effective e-safety practices, pupils must also be aware of the more nuanced digital etiquette of interacting with others online so as not to instigate problems themselves. In this book I have used the term 'e-savvy' to describe the combined aim of being safe and responsible when using digital technology.

Coding

The introduction of coding has been the biggest change in moving from an ICT curriculum to computing. The previous curriculum included aspects of 'controlling technology', but there was no direct mention of programming. Coding is now the dominant strand and makes up nearly half of the programme of study. This represents a departure from a largely consumer-based curriculum to one where pupils are the designers and creators. Whereas most teachers will have used typing and spreadsheet programs, or taken photos and videos on their phones, many will have little experience of coding. Learning to code is enjoyable for most learners but it will take an investment of your time. It is useful to view learning programming in a similar way to learning a foreign language; and there are many different programming languages you could introduce in your school. In this book, I will guide you through what you need to know to keep one virtual step ahead of your pupils. It is important to remember that designing useful code also takes logical thinking and more than a little creativity!

A few bits, bobs and bytes – some words of advice and insight

Culture

Computers are just for playing games, right? Many of your pupils will think so, and it may be a cultural shift for both the pupils and their parents to change that perception of computing. While there is nothing inherently wrong with playing computer games in the classroom, it is the learning gained from the games that is paramount.

It's logical, Captain.

Computers do what you tell them to do, so be careful what you 'say' to them. Programming is essentially a list of commands that are executed one after the other at billions of operations per second. Getting into this sequential way of thinking can be difficult for us messy, multi-directional humans, although most pupils are wonderfully more messy and multi-directional than the rest of us. Coders need to develop linear thinking and decompose tasks into tiny steps, while maintaining the creative impulse and overview that comes from exploring many possibilities and solutions at once. This linear thinking can be difficult for young learners to grasp, so cite lots of concrete examples.

In my own teaching, I have drawn inspiration from Heath Robinson – a cartoonist who designed ridiculously complicated machines to produce farcically simple outcomes, where every stage and component of the computing 'production line' acts in turn. Teachers may also like to cite Indiana Jones or Goonies-style booby traps or Wallace and Gromit contraptions instead. The point is that an initial trigger sets the processes in motion one after the other, like dominoes.

Pupil experts

Some of your pupils may be more able in certain areas of computing than you are so it's important to accept it. That is not to say that you have nothing to teach them but you need to acknowledge that we are all always learning and you will do it together. Use the pupils' expertise when you can and encourage collaborative learning in class. You could perhaps appoint children as 'digital leaders' within your school to foster the sharing of skills and to improve digital learning opportunities across the school.

Oooops!

In life, mistakes happen – but speaking from experience as the technically-minded go-to member of staff who has spent hours trying to retrieve lost files for colleagues or pupils, forgetting to save work shouldn't be one of them.

Save often! Save labelled versions and back up on separate storage.

Mistakes do happen – so love your *undo* button. It allows you to try things out, take risks and experiment with a safety net.

Reception and beyond – starting out with computing

As children begin learning about computing formally at primary school for the first time, the digital experience of individuals will vary greatly. Some children will have started learning about digital technology in Reception. Many will have been exposed to the repetitive strains of a certain gaming phenomenon where vexed birds are used as slingshot ammunition, or will have watched videos of their cute animal of choice playing the piano or skateboarding. In contrast to these who have been learning from digital devices from a young age, there will be others who instead have very limited experience of using digital technology. As with any cohort and subject area, the teacher will need to cater for and push forward the learning of every child, from whatever their initial starting point may be.

The teacher's first steps are:

- To find out what the children know and can already do
- To ascertain what devices, software and restrictions they have to work with
- To know what pupils should be learning in subsequent years.

Assessment can be a laborious task, but most pupils have an affinity with digital technology; whilst using technology shouldn't be a rarity in your classroom, there may be an opportunity at the beginning of the year to allow pupils to explore what a new or novelty device can do semi-independently, allowing you to simply observe and assess.

It is possible that pupils may not have used a particular device before, so to get a true sense of their current knowledge and skills it is important that they are offered a wide range of devices to explore.

I hope you and your class enjoy the activities in this book. Good luck on your digital journey.

Year 1 Using and understanding computing

Focus: Digital images and photography

What do I need to know?

We live in a visual world, and children today are bombarded by a wider array of visual stimuli than at any other time in history. Images have the power to move us emotionally and influence us in both positive and negative ways. The 'photoshopped' image has become synonymous with misrepresenting the real world, but digital image editing skills are essential in professional photography, art and publishing.

The National Curriculum states that pupils in KS1 should:

- *Use technology purposefully to create, organise, store, manipulate and retrieve digital content.*
- *Recognise common uses of information technology beyond school.*

Creating, editing and sharing digital images will address both of these strands.

Interesting fact

The average digital camera has around 20 megapixels, or 20 million individual coloured squares, which make the image. The human eye has the equivalent of around 576 megapixels! (Clark, 2005, clarkvision.com)

Watch **bit.ly/pricomp001** for much more detail.

Key words

Scanography (also spelled 'Scannography'): art created with a scanner.
Mash-up: putting together two or more elements to create something new.

Stage 1 Photography

Photography is as much about seeing the potential for a great shot as it is about the technology. The following activities are designed to develop both aspects of photography simultaneously. Most pupils will have experience of taking a few quick snaps but spotting or crafting the arrangement of the subjects in a shot may be a new idea. Cheese!

You will need

- Cameras, or devices that have inbuilt cameras
- Old film-based cameras (optional)
- A3 paper
- Photo frames or cardboard substitutes
- Large image printing software (e.g. **posterazor.sourceforge.net)**
- Means of transferring photos – cables, Bluetooth, cloud storage, etc.
- Device for centrally storing photos, such as a PC with plenty of storage space
- Willing photographic models and objects
- Plenty of batteries
- Real or digital exhibition space
- Digital devices for photo storage and research
- Interactive whiteboard

Getting started

If you are able to find suitable examples, show your class an old non-digital camera and film. Describe how it works: light enters the lens, inverts and is focused onto the film, which imprints a negative image through a chemical reaction with the light-sensitive layer (visit **bit.ly/pricomp002** for a detailed explanation). You may wish to extend this further by making a pinhole camera.

Explain that in digital cameras, the film has been replaced by an electronic image sensor which converts light into an electric signal. (For a full explanation, search on **howstuffworks.com**.) Explain that the image is built using lots of squares called pixels. If you zoom in on an image you can see that it looks blocky. Watch **bit.ly/pricomp003** for a full explanation.

Class activity: Capturing photos

Getting pupils to begin to think about the reasons for choosing to frame a shot in a particular way is important. Begin by selecting a range of standard-sized photos: some of interesting scenes and a few dull images of nothing much in particular. Glue each one to the middle of a large sheet of A3 paper.

Distribute these pieces of paper to individuals or groups of two, and ask the pupils to sketch the missing part of the image – the area around the photo – on to the paper. Some children will draw elaborate pictures while others will have simpler or more sparse drawings.

Once complete, use the pupils' drawings to begin a discussion about why the photographer chose to focus on a particular area of the image. You could ask:

- Does that mean the area outside the shot did not have anything of interest?
- Why do you think this particular shot was chosen?
- Could you zoom in further and still create a good photo?

Photograph a busy image, such as a street scene, an outdoor market, or even another classroom or the staffroom which has been specially decorated for the occasion, and display the image on your interactive whiteboard. You could also print out a large image to digitally stitch together with tools such as **posterazor.sourceforge.net** or buy a poster that has busy artwork, such as *Where's Wally*? Ask the class to draw cropping lines around scenes that might make interesting stand-alone photos and ask pupils why each one would make a good photo. Explore how landscape and portrait frames can be used.

Give pupils an empty, backless photo frame (or a rectangle of card with the middle cut out will suffice) and ask them to search for and discover three to five suitable shots around the school, which they will photograph with a real camera later. This can be completed in small groups and/or during a break time to minimise disruption to other classes. By limiting them to just three to five shots, they know they can't be snap-happy and instead must really compose their shots. Encourage them to think about including close-ups and interesting perspectives. Try to include a few portrait photos of teachers and learners as, firstly, this is an important part of photography, and secondly, it may please your head teacher if your class suggests he/she makes a suitable photographic model!

Whether you are using a digital camera or a device such as a mobile phone or tablet, ensure that your pupils are able to use the basic functions, including the zoom, focus, flash and review facilities, but discourage the use of the delete function as the class can learn from any mistakes they make. Allow the pupils time to experiment with the camera in the classroom first. If you have desktop lamps available, ask the pupils to explore what impact the level and direction of light have on the operation of the camera and the quality of the photo.

Allow each group enough time to carefully take their planned photos. Once the photos have all been taken, ask the pupils, not an adult, to electronically collate all the files in a central location, as transferring photos is an important skill that is often not taught or practised at school. You may wish the children to rename the image files as their own name plus a number so the photographer can be easily identified later. If the images are being imported from multiple devices, be sure not to overwrite images that share the same file name. Cull any photos of feet and ceilings (unless they are particularly picturesque examples!) but keep poor examples of deliberate shots to ask what went wrong and how they could have been improved.

To finish, print or use a device to display some anonymous examples of photos from your class collection and, in groups, ask the pupils to browse and discuss the photos taken by other children. They should talk about elements they like and dislike, and how the photo could be improved. Ask each pupil to select their favourite image from the photos they took for a real or online exhibition for the school community to view.

Photos are a wonderful medium with which to build home-school partnerships. Cameras on computers and smartphones are ubiquitous and parents can easily share photos via the school's main email address for the office to forward on to you.

Plenary

Create a 'day in the life of…' photo archive of the school and, if possible, the wider community. Pupils should use the skills that they have learnt. Collaborate with other classes to photograph the normal school day, thinking carefully about crafting the shots and what it is important to make a record of. Carrying this out as an annual activity will create a wonderful photographic record that pupils and teachers can use in the wider curriculum.

Useful links

bit.ly/pricomp004 Contains some useful advice for children learning basic photography.
bit.ly/pricomp005 'Photography for kids' YouTube playlist.
bit.ly/pricomp006 'Teaching photograpy 101' Pinterest board.
http://iphonephotographyschool.com iPhone photography school.

Stage 2 Digital art

Being creative and adapting and improving images is an increasingly important set of skills. A few decades ago, digital art was seen as niche. These days, computer-generated images or art with a digital element is mainstream. Art can take many forms, and digital art can emulate, augment or completely transcend traditional art forms. As some art can still be created more easily and effectively through traditional means, however, we need to think carefully about what we teach. For example, drawing with a mouse is difficult and the results are often poor in comparison to hand sketches.

You will need
- A colour scanner
- Coloured paper
- Cling-film
- A variety of interesting indoor and outdoor objects
- A variety of art materials
- Devices able to access **pixlr.com** or alternatives
- Devices able to access **burner.bonanza.com**

Getting started
Your pupils probably haven't had much experience with scanners so take this opportunity to examine how they work (see **bit.ly/pricomp007**) and talk about how they are usually used. Ask the pupils to suggest uses and discuss their thoughts on the advantages and disadvantages over using a camera. Ask a few individuals to try using a scanner in its usual function to scan a document.

Class activities: Creative scanners
Scanners are a cheap, wonderfully creative, yet underused piece of equipment. Many schools I've visited have defunct printers with working scanners standing idle. Scanner art, or 'scanography', has so many fun and creative applications, and there are many examples online. Whilst scanners digitalise an image just as a camera does, they have a precise focal range meaning that the image they make is 2D. Naturally, you can make a digital copy of art that your class has made by conventional means but the scanner can also be a creative tool in itself and can even add a sense of depth to a 2D image. A great place to start is to scan flowers and other objects from nature, taking inspiration from the traditional technique of pressing flowers.

> **Safety first:** Scanners are usually designed for paper so if you are putting anything else on the scanner plate it is advised to put a layer of cling film onto the plate first to prevent scratching and protect it from dirt. You do not need to close the scanner lid to be able to use it but it is sensible not to look directly at the light.

Invite a few individuals to gently place their hand on the plate of a scanner and explore the interesting images they can make. Next, ask a number of pupils to place their hands on the plate at the same time and explore overlapping the hands.

Collect a range of interesting objects from the classroom or the outdoor environment so the children can explore creating patterns using the scanner. Fallen autumn leaves, coloured pencil shavings, rows of coloured pencils, glitter, sequins or coloured sand can all make interesting patterns. Even emptying the contents of a pupil's tray or bag can make an interesting and informative work of art.

Ask the pupils to create a landscape scene using cut or ripped coloured paper and any additional art or everyday materials you have available, e.g. cling film for water, cotton wool for clouds or snow. For the best effect, ensure that the 'distant' layers of the background are a little further away from the scanner plate – this makes a blurring effect. You could achieve this by using thicker materials such as corrugated cardboard. Suggest the pupils then redesign their scene to represent a different time of day or year. For example, they could change the sky to a yellow for sunrise or black for night, and change objects in the foreground, such as the leaves on trees to reflect the different seasons. Prompt the pupils to think carefully about what needs to be changed and which elements will stay in place on the scanner.

There are endless ideas you can try and it is important that you do experiment – remember, your cheap scanner can be replaced if the worst should happen!

Class activities: Hand-drawn digital images
There isn't a barrier between traditional art and computer-generated art. It's all art! Many digital pieces of art do in fact include an element of non-digital sketching which is then digitised and augmented.

Ask your pupils to sketch a drawing on a topic you are studying in class or about something they are interested in. Scan their drawings into the computer and edit the sketch in an editing suite such as **pixlr.com** to change the image if needed. Cut away any unwanted sections using tools like **burner.bonanza.com**, then transfer the images to any program that allows layering of images such as Microsoft Word™ or PowerPoint™ to add a background and other objects into the foreground.

Plenary
Challenge your pupils to translate a design from a standard image to a scanned version. The images could include: creating a world/local map or a pirate treasure map using yellow sand, blue-dyed sand and other small objects; making a portrait of members of staff using layered paper; designing a starscape image by creating a star constellation for the background (accurately cut out holes in black paper and place transparent coloured sweet wrappers or film behind), and with your spaceship of choice in the foreground. These are just some ideas – the choice is yours! Add extra challenge by imposing a time limit. Then send the result to their parents by email at the end of the day.

Useful links

scannography.org and **bit.ly/pricomp008** Examples of Scanner Art.

Drawing and painting

Until recently, drawing using computers was not a useful activity in primary schools because the technology wasn't yet in place. While Microsoft Paint™ had many uses, pupils were not able to translate their ideas into reality using a mouse and drawing with pencil and paper was always superior. However, the introduction of touchscreen technology has changed this. While traditional methods still usually produce better results, given the average dexterity of a primary school child, drawing and painting activities are now a viable option.

Checklist

1. Wherever possible, use a touchscreen device or an e-whiteboard for a more natural painting or drawing experience.

2. For arty activities, choose an application or website that allows textured drawing. Try the following which all have similar intuitive tools such as brushes and a colour palette:
   Fresh Paint™ for Windows **microsoft.com/freshpaint**
   - Adobe Photoshop Sketch for iPad **bit.ly/pricomp009**
   - Inspire Pro for iPad **bit.ly/pricomp010**
   - Paper for iPad **bit.ly/pricomp011**
   - Infinite Painter app for Android **bit.ly/pricomp012**
   - Sumo Paint via web browser **sumopaint.com**

3. Consider using digital drawing and painting over traditional methods if:
   - the time allotted for the activity prohibits setting up and tidying up at the end
   - the environment is not conducive to painting, for example, painting scenes and objects while outside of the classroom in the school grounds or on field trips
   - the image produced is going to be used further on a computer, for example, if you plan to add it to a blog or manipulate the image using image-editing software.

Stage 3 Manipulating images

There are a myriad of different ways an image can be manipulated, from simple colour and lighting enhancement to creating a mash-up of graphics to create fantastical scenes. There are also many different digital tools to help you do it. The native photo editor that comes with the latest version of Windows has some great functions. For the full range of activities you will need software like Paint.NET, and it is this program to which I am referring in this section although many tools across many devices will have similar functions. You will be amazed at how much Year 1 pupils can do with these tools.

You will need
- Image-editing software and devices:
  - Paint.NET for Windows **getpaint.net**
  - Pixlr via web browser, Android or Apple device **pixlr.com**
  - iPiccy via web browser **ipiccy.com/editor**
  - SnapSeed for Android, iPad and iPhone **bit.ly/pricomp013**
- A photo of you (or a willing victim!)
- Tilt-shift maker and examples **tiltshiftmaker.com**
- A thick skin while your pupils turn you into an alien

Getting started
Before the lesson, find an improbable image, for example, search for 'shark with wings' or 'bear in space'. Talk to the pupils about the authenticity of the image and how it was made. Set up the idea for the 'unmasking the alien' activity that follows by letting it slip that you are an alien, and this is what 'sharks' or 'bears' look like on your planet.

Class activities: Unmasking the alien
You're an alien and your pupils have found you out! Provide the children with a digital photo of you and explain that the pupils are going to adapt the photo to show your 'natural' alien appearance as it would be back on your own planet. Make sure the background of the image has a range of objects, preferably of different colours. It is a good idea to give the pupils multiple copies of the image so they can start again from scratch with different tools.

Firstly, ask the pupils to explore changing the colour of the picture by altering the hue or filter settings (*Adjustments* menu > *Hue*). The children will have great fun turning you from green to blue to purple. They will probably have changed the colouring of the whole image. Ask them how they could just change your colour rather than the background. Prompt them towards using the *Selection* tools and specifically the *Lasso select* tool from the sidebar to draw a selected area around the item that they wish to recolour.

Ask the pupils to select a colour from the colour palette window (press *F8* on your keyboard to view the *Colours* window) and use the *Recolour* tool from the sidebar to do a similar thing again to an object in the background of the image, which is to be your spaceship parked in the distance. Ensure that they experiment with the *Tolerance* settings to change the variety of colours that are recoloured.

Next, instruct the pupils to use the *Lasso select* tool again, together with the *Cut* function (*Edit* menu > *Cut*) to cut away the extra parts of the background, leaving just the alien and spaceship.

Introduce the idea of layers (images over images) to the class. Add a layer to the alien images by pressing *F4* on your keyboard to view the *Layers* window and look for the button with the green plus sign. You will now have two pictures sharing the same canvas, with the blank image on top. Find the *Gradient* tool from the sidebar and ask the children to select two colours from the colour palette window and drag a gradient across the image. The top, blank layer should turn into a blurring of the two colours and cover the alien image. On the *Layer* window, use the up and down arrows to move the alien image to the foreground. You should now have an image of the alien and the spaceship with a colourful alien world background.

Class activities: Having an effect

Using the photos taken by the pupils in Stage 1 (p2), or using other interesting images, ask the children to explore the *Effects* menu. Prompt the pupils to make the photo look like a piece of art using the *Artistic* settings (*Effects > Artistic*). Encourage the pupils to tweak and improve from the default settings to create an interesting image. Using a photo portrait of someone, encourage the pupils to explore using the tools in the *Photo* menu (*Effects > Photo*) to add glow, remove red-eye and create other effects.

Class activities: Tilt to make tiny

Blurriness often spoils a photo but it can also be used to add interesting effects to an image. One pleasing effect is called tilt-shift. Essentially, this effect makes a scene appear like a tiny toy version.

Explain to the pupils that the alien overlord (you) plans to shrink the Earth so it will fit into your spaceship but you want to know how it will look first using the tilt-shift effect. The pupils will need a distant photo of an outdoor space looking down from above at a gentle angle of approximately 30–60°. Search online for tilt-shift photos and videos or visit **tiltshiftmaker.com** for a better idea of what this looks like. It is important not to have anything in the immediate foreground, and objects should be some distance away from the camera to allow the illusion to work. The pupils will need to decide where they want to focus the viewer's attention, for example, at street level where the scene is busy. This section is to remain unblurred. Use the *Rectangle select* tool from the sidebar and select approximately the top ten percent of the image, then blur it using the *Unfocus* tool (*Effects > Blurs*). Next, select the top twenty percent of the image, which includes the original ten percent you have already blurred, and use the *Unfocus* tool again. Repeat until you reach the chosen area of interest, which will remain unblurred. You will therefore have a graduation of blurriness from not at all, to mildly blurred, to very blurred on the top edge. Do the same for the bottom of the image. The result should look like a miniature toy version of the scene.

Plenary

Ask the pupils to build a miniature city using Lego™, play-dough or other items. When it is complete, help them to take a photo of their city from an angle of approximately 30–60°. Once the photo has been transferred to a computer, open your image-editing software and add additional items in the area of interest, such as hand-drawn and scanned sketches as discussed in Stage 2 (p4) or cut-out images of classmates. Edit the image by recolouring and cropping and then make it into another tilt-shift image.

Useful links

bit.ly/pricomp014 Tutorials on using Paint.NET.
bit.ly/pricomp015 and **bit.ly/pricomp016** Examples of tilt-shift.

Progression

Your pupils will now have basic skills in using a digital camera purposefully to capture crafted scenes, people and objects and store them ready to edit or share. They will have the skills to improve and manipulate images for a variety of uses, including making art. Each of these skills is vital to modern computing and we will make use of these skills again and again throughout the rest of the computing curriculum.

Cross-curricular links

The links to other curriculum areas are limited only by the imagination and skill needed to create them. Here are just a few ideas to get you started: creating a stimulus or illustrating creative writing in English; creating images of ideas and principles in science and maths; using and enhancing archived photos in history; visualising and editing prototypes in design and technology.

Year 1 e-Savvy

Focus: Finding, using and understanding online images

What do I need to know?

Striking a balance between keeping children informed about the potential dangers of the online world and not filling them with perpetual fear is not easy, especially as they set out on their digital learning journeys. Whatever your views on when it is appropriate for children to start using the Internet, the reality is that some children in a Year 1 class will already be active online.

The National Curriculum states that pupils in KS1 should:
• *Use technology safely and respectfully, keeping personal information private; identify where to go for help and support when they have concerns about content or contact on the internet or other online technologies.*

In Year 1, we will focus on keeping personal information private, and respectful use of the things other users share and donate to the web.

> ### Interesting fact
>
> An estimated 1.8 billion digital images are uploaded to social media every single day. That's more in two minutes than the total number of photos that existed worldwide 150 years ago[1].

Key words

Digital legacy: The trail of information we leave online and on old devices, which remains live for a long time.
Creative Commons: A system by which creators of media can give varying degrees of permission for others to reuse their work.
Photoshopped: Coined from the popular image-editing suite but now refers to any manipulated image.

---

1 Source: www.slideshare.net/kleinerperkins/internet-trends-2014-05-28-14-pdf/62 & www.theatlantic.com/technology/archive/2015/11/how-many-photographs-of-you-are-out-there-in-the-world/413389/

Stage 1 The basics

By encouraging positive habits from the very beginning of your pupils' education with regard to how to stay safe and by savvy online, and by linking as much as possible to the offline world, you will be able to prevent many problems arising in the first place. The first step is to highlight the need to exercise caution when sharing personal information in the public space that is the web.

You will need
- A mock 'top-secret diary' with interesting entries
- An adult to collude with
- A collection of images of people (including children)
- A collection of 'personal information' statements
- Sheets of A3 paper (enough for one per child) and scissors
- An interactive whiteboard

Getting started
Begin by talking about privacy and what this means to the pupils. Discuss the different levels of privacy:
- Inner privacy – things only you know
- Family privacy – things only your family know about you
- Friend privacy – things your friends know about you
- Community privacy – things that everyone who knows you might know about you.

Ask the pupils to categorise the privacy level of a few examples using an 'imaginary friend' that you have invented as the subject.

Class activities: Diary confessions
Collude with another member of staff to set up a situation in which the class are poised to start writing a 'friend privacy-level' diary. For this occasion, you have brought in your own 'top-secret' diary. You show the pupils the diary but explain that you do not intend to share the contents with them as it is private. However, you get called away from the classroom and you absent-mindedly pass the diary to a member of staff nearby (who you are in collusion with), and then rush out of the room, leaving the member of staff holding the diary. After a few moments, the staff member begins leafing through the diary, making sure that the pupils have noticed with some well-timed chuckles and gasps. The member of staff should then begin to read sections of the hoax diary, such as:

> *10th September*
>
> *I thought that I had been caught for a moment today. One of the children walked in just as I was removing them from the classroom. If anyone discovers I have a mortal fear of red pencils, my career as a teacher will be over. I wonder if anyone knows that's why there are fewer red pencils than any other colour. One day I will be brave enough to remove them all. Horrid things!*

16th September

My third letter to the Oxford English Dictionary has been sent back. It seems they didn't like my suggestion to make b and d interchangeable and stop using full stops to save marking. Looks like the children will just have to learn how to use them after all.

Make sure that you have added your own zany diary entries.

You then return to the classroom and ask what has been going on. Allow the pupils to drop the member of staff in it and be 'teacher cross' ('*That has made me very sad*') with the member of staff and say that it is wrong to peep at things they know are private. The member of staff should retort that you should not have left your private information in public. Discuss with the pupils who is right. Make it clear at this point that the children's red pencils are safe and that the whole situation was set up. Make the connection between what has been discussed so far and posting information on the web.

Ask the children to suggest pieces of information that can be plotted on the line below.

Secret facts	Friend facts	Safe facts
Things I don't want anyone to know	Things only friends should know	Things anyone can know

Figure 1A: Secrecy line

Here are some ideas of the things they might include and where you could place them:
- First name (safe fact)
- The name of the school you go to (friend fact)
- That you went to see a movie at 2pm last Saturday (safe fact)
- That you are going to see a movie at 2pm next Saturday (friend fact)
- You are afraid of the dark (secret fact)
- Your birthday (friend fact)
- That you like spaghetti (safe fact)
- That your older brother/sister once fooled you into eating a dog biscuit (secret fact)
- You don't like parties but pretend you do (secret fact)
- Your telephone number (friend fact)
- Your photo (friend fact).

Don't go into details about the darker side of the web with a KS1 class, beyond the 'stranger danger' message that we give about the offline world to children of this age. If anyone they do not know in the offline world asks for personal information, they shouldn't tell them or even talk to them and should tell an adult about the request.

Class activities: Best face forward
Take a piece of A3 paper for each child and cut a face-sized circular hole in the centre of the paper. Ask the pupils to write and/or draw ideas of 'safe facts' on one side of the paper, including examples about themselves. Then ask them to turn their paper over and write some 'friend facts' on the other side.

Ask a third of the class to 'wear' their facts by holding their sheet of paper up to their face and looking through the hole, while the rest of the pupils look at what they have written – repeat for both sides. If anyone wishes to change the position of a fact, for example, change from a 'safe fact' to a 'friend fact', ask them to circle the fact in pencil. Repeat the activity twice more with the other two thirds of the class. Ask for some volunteers to be 'live marked' in front of the class by you. Use a black marker pen to cross out any information on the safe fact side of the picture that should really be 'friend fact' or secret.

Discuss whether adding an image of themselves online is a safe thing to share. After you have vetted the information you can display the 'safe' side of the paper turned outwards on a window, showing the 'friend' side inside the classroom to emphasise the point. Discuss the fact that this doesn't just apply to oneself but that you shouldn't add images or personal information about other people on the web either, especially in public areas.

Discuss why contact details, specific personal information and future plans shouldn't be shared with people you don't know in the offline world, for example:
- This kind of information can be used to track individuals to a location and know when they will not be at home.
- Strangers can use specific information to suggest that they know you in some way, e.g. 'Hi Becky, I'm a friend of a friend and I've heard it's your birthday tomorrow.'

There are degrees of being public and private on the web, but no information shared online can be guaranteed to remain private. Security experts often say that humans are the biggest flaw in the armour when it comes to technology security. Information can be found via lost phones and memory sticks, hacks via weak passwords, and even friends falling out and making information, which was shared in confidence, public as a friendship turns sour. Talk about only sharing, whether in public or in private, what you will not regret later. Furthermore, discuss about 'digital legacy', or the idea that what is put on the web will potentially stay there forever.

Finish by briefly relating this to bullying and unkindness. If the children are concerned that images or information, whether true or untrue, are viewable online they should seek the help of an adult.

Plenary
Before the lesson, download images of people, including some children, and write captions to go with each image that disclose varying degrees of private information. In pairs, ask the pupils to sort the images and sentences into whether they are 'safe' or 'unsafe' things to post online, and explain their reasoning.

Useful links

thinkuknow.co.uk/5_7 A fun way for children to learn about Internet safety.

Stage 2 Savvy with images

Have you ever taken something that doesn't belong to you? In the pursuit of making better, more presentable resources for your class, it is likely you have! Before you begin to teach pupils to be savvy when using the web, take a look at what you do yourself. It is easy to become a copyright infringer without realising it, copying and pasting into your class resources without a second thought. It is easy to stay legal and we owe it to our children to practise what we preach and be responsible users of the web.

You will need
- An old classroom display
- Another teacher to collude with
- A collection of manipulated images, such as **bit.ly/pricomp017**
- Devices with access to a search engine
- Devices with access to **search.creativecommons.org**

Getting started
Begin by talking about ownership. Use the example of stationery. A pupil may own a pencil case with a picture of a cartoon character on the lid, but how far does that ownership go? They can attempt to sketch a copy of the cartoon character, but are they allowed to copy it in other ways?

Class activities: Stolen images
Firstly, collude with another teacher and prime them to enter your classroom while your class is just getting started and begin to 'borrow' one of your class displays by hastily removing it from the wall (preferably one that you want to replace anyway!). Ask the obvious questions: 'What do you think you are doing?' and 'Where are you taking my display?' The teacher should respond that they think the work is so nice that they want to display it in their classroom.

Ask the children to think of reasons why the other teacher shouldn't do this. The idea of property and 'it's not yours' should be among the arguments put forward. Prompt the pupils to develop this idea. Invite the teacher back into the classroom and allow the pupils to explain why the teacher can't have the display. The teacher can make counter-arguments to develop the idea further but finally the teacher agrees to return 'a' display. The original display should be brought back into the class but with some images having been replaced by some funny images, such as photos of volunteers pulling funny faces.

Confess to the class that the role play was a set-up and put the altercation into the context of online images. Ask whether, like the teacher and the class display, anyone can simply take any image they find from an image search or website, and discuss whether the images belong to someone. Say that the images of funny faces that have been added to your classroom display represent the unsuitable images that can be found on the web, and let them know that search engines have a safe search filter which will stop images that are not suitable from being shown. It is important that the children know that they can tell an adult when they see something they don't like or they find disturbing without fear of being in trouble.

Class activities: Fact or fake?

Search **Pinterest.com** for a range of interesting but not manipulated images to accompany the photoshopped image collection at **bit.ly/pricomp017**. Ask the children to identify which images are real and which are fake. Make sure they realise that, in real life, the edits are usually more subtle than this. Talk about strategies for identifying real from fake in a world where any image can be created. Discuss the context of the image and whether it matters that an image isn't real. Talk about the role of authoritative and trusted sites – reliable organisations that are likely to have checked the origin of the image before adding it to their site, such as the BBC. Often, using a website is like getting to know a person. You begin with a friendly but healthy scepticism, and the site will either earn your trust over time or disappoint you.

Class activities: Searching, hunting and using

Not all search engines are the same. Most of the famous search engines are very similar but with subtle differences. For example, does clicking a searched image expand to a larger preview or does it take you to a site where the image is hosted, thus potentially exposing your device to unfriendly software? Just because a search result is near the top of the list, this doesn't mean it is friendly. Before you allow pupils to explore the browser, ensure that you know every aspect of how it behaves, so you can talk your class through it. You should also allow pupils to explore a few different search engines as they will probably be exposed to a variety of them at home.

Ask the pupils to conduct an image search on the search engine of your choice. It's important that you are searching for a specific reason, so consider what you are doing in other curriculum areas and how the images will be used. You may wish to vet the search results for the terms you intend to use first, to make sure the material is suitable and of interest. Point out the main features of the search engine:

- Search bar
- Categories – web, images, videos, etc.
- Search tools – additional options

Highlight the fact that the school uses a safe search filter to help them find things relevant to their age group. It is important to explain that the safe search is not completely secure, and that the children still need to be web savvy when using it.

Savvy image searchers should follow these guidelines:

- Only view images within the search engine – they should not, at this stage, click through to the host site unless instructed to do so by an adult
- If they see an image that is inappropriate, they can choose to ignore it or tell an adult if they find it distressing – they certainly shouldn't point it out to their classmates
- They should not download an image unless an adult gives permission and the image licensing rights allow us to do so.

Ask the pupils to experiment with the *Image search* tools, which give you more options to refine the image search features. Include searching for a particular size of image, colour of image or type of image.

Set up an image hunt. Before the lesson, enter simple search terms into the search engine and bookmark a suitable image for which you feel the children will be able to guess which terms you entered. Display the image on the class whiteboard and ask the children to hunt for the image by guessing the search terms. You can award points or rewards for the first searchers to find it. You can also use search tool filters, such as searching for a particular colour of image, to make the task more intricate.

Take some suggestions of which images the children would like to download. Talk about who owns the image. In most cases the images will belong to the creator of the image (and not 'Mr. Google', as a Year 2 child once told me!). Ask whether they would be happy for you to use their image without permission, relating this back to the role play altercation about the display (p14).

Discuss why the image creator might or might not wish to openly share the image. Use the analogy of a shop window. The shopkeeper may wish you to see the goods in the window, but that doesn't mean you can run off with them. Discuss how using your own images on your own website, or giving a limited number of people permission, doesn't mean that everyone has permission to use them.

Ask the pupils to brainstorm ideas about how the image author could indicate that they are willing to openly share the image. Introduce the idea of 'Creative Commons' licences – the system by which creators of media can give varying degrees of permission for others to reuse their work. The pupils don't need to know the details at this stage, but for your own information you can read more at **creativecommons.org/licenses**.

Either find the licence filter on your search engine of choice or use **search. creativecommons.org** image search to discover images that the children can use.

Plenary

Ask the children to design a simple poster using Creative Commons images they have found, together with just a few words to highlight how to be a savvy searcher. Either print images and complete offline, or import the images into a suitable software program (e.g. Microsoft Word or Excel™) by saving the images to the computer and then dragging them from the folder into place.

Useful links

copyrightandschools.org Copyright information site.

lifehacker.com/follow-this-chart-to-know-if-you-can-use-an-image-from-1615584870
A useful flow diagram showing whether to use an image.

pixabay.com Creative Commons images.

Progression

The children have learnt how to conduct safe and legal image searching and have looked at how images can be edited in both useful but also negative ways. They have also thought about image manipulation and whether images can be trusted.

Cross-curricular links

There are many links to social and emotional development and the ideas of sharing and taking images without the owner's permission. In addition, altered images have clear links with art, but also history, as edited images have always been used in propaganda and historians must look closely at evidence to decide whether something is a primary source.

Year 1 Coding

Focus: The basics and movement

What do I need to know?

Coding is increasingly becoming a required skill, and encouraging young children to become interested in computer science is essential. Yet writing lots of lines of code isn't always appealing, especially when one hidden mistake can mean that the end result, instead of being the next big thing, simply doesn't work. Luckily there are lots of resources designed for young learners that have jigsaw-like blocks of code to snap together for easy and quickly satisfying results. Coding is a design process that requires logic and a great deal of experiment, failure and improvement, and it is essential for your pupils to develop a 'let's see what this does' attitude to coding.

The National Curriculum states that pupils in KS1 should:

- *Understand what algorithms are; how they are implemented as programs on digital devices; and that programs execute by following precise and unambiguous instructions.*
- *Create and debug simple programs.*
- *Use logical reasoning to predict the behaviour of simple programs.*

The pupils will cover all of these elements in this section, with a particular focus on debugging and furthering their knowledge of algorithms.

> ### Interesting fact
>
> Current computer processors commonly have around half a trillion transistors on them! A decade ago, the number was around half a billion... that's a thousandfold increase in just ten years.[2]

Key words

Algorithm: An ordered list of commands for a computer to execute one by one until it is completed, stopped or interrupted by another process.
Variables: An element of code that can change its value to give different inputs to other pieces of code.
Decomposition: Breaking big or complex tasks into small step-by-step components for a computer to understand.

---

2 Source: https://en.wikipedia.org/wiki/Transistor_count

Blockly system: A visual coding system as opposed to a text-based one, where draggable blocks of code connect together like a jigsaw to create an algorithm, instead of keying in text.

Sprites: Characters, props and objects that appear in computer games and programs.

Stage 1 Getting things in order

Digital technology is built with code. An algorithm is simply a list of ordered instructions that a computer follows in series, and programming is essentially writing a list of commands for the computer to respond to given an initial set of conditions and additional inputs.

You will need
- A couple of short video clips showing a sequence of actions, e.g. sport footage or fast-paced cartoons
- A 'robotic' teaching assistant
- Logic gate diagrams
- Robot head boxes
- Paper

Getting started
Invite a few pupils to recall their morning routine, and ask the rest of the class to break down each routine into steps and to write each step on a mini whiteboard. For example:
1. Get dressed
2. Eat breakfast
3. Clean teeth
4. Leave the house.

Ask the pupils to suggest alternative options/decisions for each step – for example, do they get dressed into school uniform or a onesie?

Introduce the term 'algorithm' and explain that it means a list of detailed instructions that have been written in the right order, which forms the foundation of coding. Watch the video, 'What is an algorithm?' at **bit.ly/pricomp018.**

Class activities: Narration
Show the pupils a short video clip showing a sequence of actions – sport footage or fast-paced cartoons work well. Take suggestions for what is happening on screen from the class. Invite a volunteer to watch another clip and describe what happens to the rest of the class, who are turned the other way so they cannot see it. Then show the clip to the whole class and discuss which details were included and which were omitted by the pupil who narrated it.

Ask the pupils to practise self-narration. For example, ask the children to be commentators for their own sporting skills. This activity is best completed outside the classroom as it will be noisy.

Class activities: Robot children
Explain that the pupils are going to be robots who respond perfectly to your voice commands. Ask them to do various tasks around the classroom, taking the opportunity

to make them tidy up the classroom for a change in the process. Then, introduce your 'robotic' teaching assistant, TA1000, who has been clad in tinfoil. Explain to pupils that they themselves are much cleverer robots than TA1000, who has to have each task broken down into tiny steps. Ask TA1000 to do something simple, following step-by-step instructions – making a sandwich is a classic example that is often used in instructional writing lessons; painting a picture or making something out of play-dough are possibilities too. Ensure that you include lots of imprecise instructions that your robot can misunderstand with comic results, and ask your pupils to offer better directions.

Ask the pupils to work in small groups. They should choose one of their group to wear a robot head – a spacious cardboard box that will block their view, but to avoid health and safety concerns, will allow them to still be able to see their own feet to prevent tripping. The rest of the group should control their robot to do certain tasks, thinking very carefully about the steps involved and giving step-by-step commands. For example, pupils could instruct their robot to copy an unseen picture based on their descriptions, or drive a remote control car around an assault course following their instructions.

Class activities: Logic gates

Using an open space such as the school hall, set up a logic flow diagram similar to the one shown below, using mini whiteboards, mats, skipping ropes and other PE equipment.

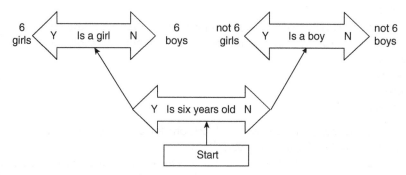

Figure 1B: Logic flow diagram

Ask the pupils to walk through their logical path to sort themselves into four groups. You may wish to introduce the binary symbols of 1 and 0 to replace Y and N respectively. Inside a computer's processor, the number 1 means the transistor gate is open, whereas the number 0 means it is closed.

In small teams, instruct the pupils to create their own logic diagrams using their own criteria. Once completed, ask the groups to circulate and try each other's logic diagrams.

Create a new logic flow diagram, or modify your original diagram to include some commands. See the example on the next page.

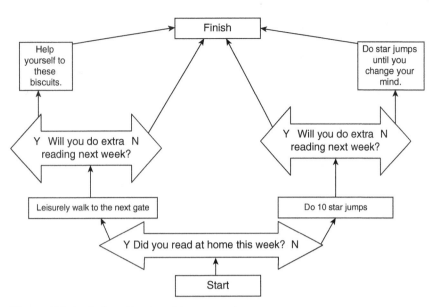

Figure 1C: Logic flow diagram with commands

Instruct the children to make their own logic flow diagrams with commands and get the other groups to try them out as before. If you are able, try to connect as many of the individual diagrams together to make a huge, complex diagram for the children to navigate.

Plenary
In small groups, ask your pupils to design a logic gate board game with commands similar to the logic flow diagram with commands above, using paper and a counter or coin they can flip to generate Y/N or 1/0 choices. Once completed, the pupils can try the creations from other groups.

Useful links

bit.ly/pricomp19 BBC: What is an algorithm?

Stage 2 Starting to move

Controlling the movement of objects or 'sprites' is the foundation of programming. Telling an object to move forwards or backwards, turn left or right, or appear at a given set of coordinates is fairly simple, but creating a linear set of instructions for these takes patience and a lot of experimentation.

You will need
- Chinese instructions **bit.ly/pricomp020**
- 'What is code?' video **bit.ly/pricomp21**
- A floor robot such as Ozobot, Sphero, Bee-Bot and/or similar devices
- Daisy the Dinosaur iPad app **daisythedinosaur.com**
- Lightbot for browser **hourofcode.com/LB**
- Run Marco! Coding adventure game for browser **allcancode.com**
- ScratchJr for iPad and Android **scratchjr.org**
- Squared paper

Getting started
So far, the pupils have learnt about algorithms as a set of instructions in pictorial form but they have yet to see real coding. Watch the video 'What is code?' at **bit.ly/pricomp21**. Introduce the pupils to the idea of there being many different coding languages, just like there are many different languages in the world and perhaps even in your classroom.

Here is a set of instructions in simplified Chinese. Your pupils speak at least one language but are they able to read this using only the vocabulary given below? Ask the children to do as the instructions ask once they have understood them in full.

摸摸你的头
摸摸你的肩膀
摸摸你的膝盖
摸摸你的脚趾

Figure 1D: Chinese instructions

Give your pupils the following vocabulary:

你的 your　　　头 head　　　脚趾 toes

Figure 1E: Chinese words set 1

At this stage some pupils may infer the correct meaning. When learning and reading code, you will be able to work out some of the unknown elements from the parts of the code that you do know.

Now give your pupils some more vocabulary:

摸摸 touch　　　肩膀 shoulders　　　膝盖 knees

Figure 1F: Chinese words set 2

Full translation:
    Touch your head
    Touch your shoulders
    Touch your knees
    Touch your toes

Talk about how once the instructions are clear, the actions are easy to do, and how this is the same in coding. Making your instructions clear for the computer is therefore critical. Programming languages have much in common with spoken languages. Each has its own grammar, syntax and even punctuation, which can mean the difference between a program running well and an error message.

Class activities: Get moving

If you have access to an iPad, download the free Daisy the Dinosaur app **daisythedinosaur.com**. Ask the pupils to enter the *Free-play* mode to get to grips with how the app works. Instruct the pupils to complete tasks that you design or ask them to try some of the tutorial tasks. This app uses the Blockly system, draggable blocks of code that connect together like a jigsaw to create an algorithm. Point out the words 'command' and 'stage' used in this platform (go to the viewing area to observe what the code does). These are words that the children will encounter throughout their coding journey.

Log on to the Lightbot site at **hourofcode.com/LB** and choose the device you wish to work with. Choose the 'basic' levels and ask the pupils to work their way through the eight levels. Identify and promote the key terms: 'run' (same as play – begin an algorithm), 'rotate', 'actions' (such as 'jump'). The levels will require lots of trial and error. There are also a maximum of 12 commands, so the pupils will need to keep their instructions succinct.

Once the pupils have completed the first eight levels, ask them about the following: their strategy; and what was difficult; and what other abilities they would like Lightbot to have.

Now ask the pupils to explore a similar coding game, Run Marco! (**allcancode.com**) to practise movement of the sprite. This platform also uses the Blockly system of draggable connecting code.

So far, the pupils have been following instructions and completing set tasks. Use the Scratch Junior iPad and Android app via **scratchjr.org** to allow the children to create their own movement animation. Ask them to experiment with the distance number. Point out the green flag, which is the *Run* function. They will also need the *Undo* function (bottom right) and the *Reset* button so they can reset their sequence after they have viewed it – this can be found next to the flag. Instruct them to use the *Forward*, *Backward* and *Rotate blocks* functions at the very least. Encourage them to try out other functions and go beyond the baseline. Try to give them a structure to work within, perhaps based on a topic you are working on in another area of the curriculum. Once completed, ask the pupils to exhibit their creations.

Class activities: Getting physical

Coding and seeing your sprites move on the screen is satisfying and fun but it is so much more tangible for young children when their code moves physical objects. There are a range of physical devices that allow pupils to program sequences of movements: Bee-Bots are devices commonly found in primary schools but it is good practice to have a diverse range of devices (known as an ecosystem) to use in tandem, in order to broaden the children's experience and understanding of coding. Ozobot and Sphero are two more devices that can be used in a similar way to Bee-Bots.

Away from the computer, code an algorithm to move a physical device through an assault course and traverse to a particular point in one continuous sequence. This will require some trial and improvement. For an extra challenge, you can rearrange one part of the course for the children to navigate around. These changes can happen periodically every three or five minutes, depending on how difficult you wish to make the activity.

Plenary
Ask the class to design their own Lightbot level on a piece of squared paper, with numbers in the squares denoting the heights of different platforms. Ask the pupils to solve their own puzzle on a separate piece of squared paper using the same symbols as the Lightbot game: arrow, jump and lightbulb. Fold over the solved answer so it cannot be seen, and ask other children to solve the level directly under the hidden answer. You may wish to ask your pupils to write their name next to their attempt so you can assess it later. Each time, fold over the answer to hide it. Once lots of pupils have attempted to solve the puzzle, unfold the paper to reveal everyone's answers. As a class, look at the different ways (not counting wrong answers) in which the same puzzle can be solved. There is often more than one way to write code to achieve the same goals, though a coder should attempt to solve problems in the most efficient way possible.

Useful links

bit.ly/pricomp022 CBeebies coding game.

Stage 3 Moving differently

Moving smoothly through 3D (virtual) space isn't the only way to travel, and there are a variety of different methods to make your sprites move.

You will need
- A large space, for example the hall
- Two sets of large print numbers 1–6
- A magic wand and cape (optional)
- Devices able to run Scratch **scratch.mit.edu**
- Cat and mouse game **bit.ly/pricomp023**

Getting started
Working in a large space, for example the school hall, explain to the class that you're a wizard and it's time to use your powers to make the pupils do what you want. As well as being able to turn the children left and right, and moving them forward and backward, you can also make them (nearly) instantly appear at any point in the hall. (Unfortunately, your omnipotence runs short of making them know their left and right!)

Make a very simple coordinates system by affixing large numbers 1, 2 and 3 to opposite ends of the hall in one direction, and large numbers 4, 5 and 6 at opposite ends of the hall in the other direction. Use any floor markings already printed on the hall floor to your advantage, or use special magical invisible lines that the children can imagine if not.

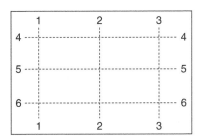

Figure 1G: Coordination system

Before starting, ensure that your *no running* spell has been cast which has the unfortunate effect of turning teachers into fire-breathing gargoyles if anyone runs around and causes a hazard. Explain that you have also used your magical powers to give the pupils the ability to (safely) bounce off walls if they run out of space. A note of caution: children seemingly bounce off the walls every time it is wet play or it is a non-uniform day, but for some reason when you give them permission to do so things can go awry, so be vigilant!

Give them commands such as:
- Walk forwards three steps
- Turn to your right
- Everyone stand on line 1
- All girls stand near point (1, 5)
- Everyone look towards the clock.

Class activities: Start scratching

This will be the first time the children will use the full version of Scratch and it will be the main platform used throughout this book. Therefore it is important for both you and your class to get to know it. Take the pupils on a tour of the platform and allow them time to experiment with its features. Emphasise the correct names for each feature whenever possible.

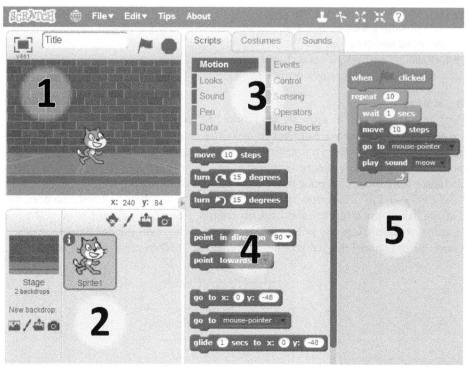

Figure 1H: Scratch layout

1. Window 1 is called the 'stage' as this is where the action happens. This is where you can view your sprites and backgrounds doing all the wonderful things you have coded them to do. Above the stage itself are three important features: the blue *Full screen* button; the *Green flag* trigger that starts the program and can initiate some of your code; and the red *Stop* button, which stops all running code.
2. Window 2 shows and manages all the resources for your design. It is split into two sections: one for your sprites and one for your backdrops. When you click on the current backdrop, the options in window 3 will change, allowing you to manage and edit the backgrounds for the stage. Sprites have slightly different settings available, with costumes and motion code being just two examples. There are four different ways to add new sprites and backdrops, corresponding to the four icon buttons (from left to right): from the sprite library; from paint; upload from the computer; take a photo with the computer's camera.
3. At the top of window 3 there are three tabs:
   - **Scripts** – This is where you will create and edit your code. Each sprite or backdrop can have code attached to it to change its behaviour. When this tab is clicked you will see in window 3 code categories with titles such as *Motion* and *Events*. There will be strings of code in coloured blocks in window 4 which can be dragged into the code editor area of window 5.
   - **Costumes/backdrops** – When you click this tab, the right-hand side of the screen will change, allowing you to edit and manage all of your backdrops, or edit the appearance of the sprite you have currently selected in window 2. The same sprite can have different appearances or *Costumes*, which you can code to change whenever you wish. For example, you may wish to alternate between two costumes with a different leg at the front to give the suggestion of walking, or wings of a bird up or down to allow flapping. You may wish to take the costumes literally and change the clothes of your sprite. You can add new costumes in the same four ways as you added your sprites (library, paint, upload, photo).
   - **Sounds** – Scratch allows users to record and upload sounds to add to your code. There is also an extensive library of sounds, which your pupils will take great delight in annoying you with unless headphones are provided.

In addition, there is a toolbar at the top of the screen with functions such as *Opening* and *Saving* work. There is also a *Sign in* option. I advise you to set up a free Scratch account for each of your pupils as this will provide an excellent record of their computer science projects when evidence is needed.

Class activities: Get a move on
In the coding we have met so far, the pupils have had only a limited range of options open to them to achieve a set goal. The possibilities in Scratch are boundless, so it is important that your pupils stay focused on their goal but how they achieve it should be up to them to decide. However, there are some basics to learn first.

As with the *Getting started* activity in the hall (p25), there are many different ways to get your sprite to move. Click on a sprite, then the *Script* tab, then *Motion* to see the strings of code shown in Figure 1i on the next page.

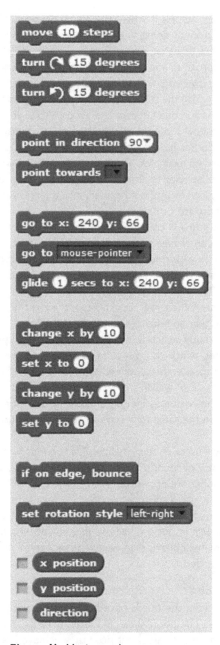

Figure 1i: Motion code

Most of these items should be fairly straightforward. Similar types of blocks are bunched together with a gap in between. Many of the blocks have numbers and drop-down boxes to select different options – these are variables, or things you can change within the code to achieve the desired goal. The final three blocks have tick boxes, which can add additional information.

Class activities: Cat and mouse

Introduce the idea of triggers – something that begins, stops or alters an algorithm. There are many different triggers in Scratch and many of them are found in the *Events* section of code. The most commonly-used trigger is the *Green flag*, which starts the program running.

Ask your pupils to experiment with the flag trigger and motion code in a cat and mouse game at **bit.ly/pricomp023**. Code the cat to catch the mouse. Encourage your class to use a range of strategies to catch the mouse and suggest that they incorporate code from the *Control* section too.

Plenary

Ask your pupils to devise a way to catch the mouse using the keyboard arrow keys and the *when* ____ *key pressed* trigger in the *Events* area. This will probably need one algorithm for each of the different keys. Show the pupils that if you right-click on the code, one of the options is to duplicate every block from that point forward.

Progression

Your pupils will now have an understanding of what coding is, the sort of features and key vocabulary involved, and the possible ways they can use it – even at the basic level they are currently at. They will understand the need for clear, ordered instructions, and they are beginning to understand how choices, variables and triggers can be used to affect the function of a program.

Cross-curricular links

All coding has links to maths and the focus on movement lends itself to work on angles, coordinates and many other aspects of shape, space and measure in the maths National Curriculum. Movement and sequence also connects well with PE, and many of the pre-computer activities have had a physical element. There is also a possible crossover with English grammar and MFL, as programming languages have syntax and rules just like other languages.

Year 2 Using and understanding computing

Focus: Sound and audio

What do I need to know?

The world is a noisy place, and not just in your classroom. We are constantly enveloped in a sea of sound, with cheeps and ringtones of digital technology being a pervasive source. Yet audio technology is an often overlooked, valuable and engaging learning tool in the classroom. The use of audio gives a voice (literally) to pupils who are not able to fully express themselves in writing. While we treasure everything every pupil says in class, it is wonderful to gather the best examples as audio recordings to share and use as evidence.

The National Curriculum for England states that pupils in KS1 should:

- *Use technology purposefully to create, organise, store, manipulate and retrieve digital content.*
- *Recognise common uses of information technology beyond school.*

Recording, editing and publishing audio covers both of these strands.

Because recording audio by its nature is a loud activity, I strongly suggest considering relocating to a more sound-dampening place, or ask pupils to complete the recording activities one group at a time.

Interesting fact

The earliest known audio recording of the human voice was made in 1860 by Édouard-Léon Scott de Martinville, and you can hear it at **bit.ly/pricomp024**.

Key words

Diaphragm: a thin membrane that moves in response to or to generate sound waves in devices like microphones and speakers.

Stage 1 Open mic

I could never be a DJ. It seems that almost every adult dislikes hearing themselves on audio recordings, yet children seem to love it.

Knowing a little about sound and how microphones and speakers work can give your pupils a good practical knowledge that will aid their recording technique. In this section, the pupils will begin to make audio recordings with a variety of methods and on different devices.

You will need
- An old traditional handheld microphone
- An old speaker
- Examples of old music media and devices
- Cling film
- A cardboard tube from a roll of kitchen towel
- Rubber bands
- Devices able to record digital audio
- How speakers work bit.ly/pricomp025
- AudioBoom audioboom.com
- Sound around you app for iPad **soundaroundyou.com**
- Google Maps **www.google.co.uk/maps**

Getting started

Microphones come in many different shapes and sizes, but most share a common feature: a 'diaphragm'. This is a thin barrier that moves back slightly as a sound wave compression hits it; it has a similar function to a human eardrum. After this point, many different technologies are used, such as crystals and condensers, to change the sound and movement energy into electrical signals. Show your class a traditional handheld microphone. Strip away as many of the protective layers around the head of the microphone as you dare, in order to show the children the inner workings.

A speaker works in a similar way, but in reverse. Often a magnet is used to make a diaphragm move rapidly, which causes compression waves in the air. It would aid your explanation if you are able to take an old speaker apart and show the children the inner workings. Alternatively, see the video at **bit.ly/pricomp025** for more details.

Take a cardboard tube from a roll of kitchen towel, apply a layer of slightly stretchy cling film over the end and fix this in place with a rubber band. In pairs, ask the pupils to take it in turns to speak into the cling film while their partner watches. It may be easier to see the cling film move if the tube is angled so that light reflects from the surface of the film. For best effects, encourage the children to adopt a whistling mouth shape and make low, resonating sounds. The cling film will move in part due to the child's breathing as well as sounds waves, so you may like to try the same thing using music from a speaker to move the cling film.

Class activities: Record attempts

Audio storage has changed a lot over the years, from Edison's wax phonograph cylinders, which resembled candles, via vinyl gramophones and turntables, cassettes, CDs and minidiscs, to digital music files such as the mp3. Now even the mp3 is being superseded by audio streaming services. Show the pupils as many examples of old audio recording devices as possible and allow them to explore and ask questions.

Every mobile phone, tablet and computer now comes with a microphone, so you will have a range of devices at your disposal. Locate the recording software on your device, often called *Voice recorder* or *Voice memo*, and open the app. In small groups, practise recording, saving, playing and deleting audio within the app. Ask the pupils to improve the quality of the voice recordings. Suggest they try to optimise their distance from the microphone: close enough to be heard well, but not so close to cause distortion. If the device is portable they can attempt, with supervision, to seek a quieter location. Otherwise, placing a coat over their head can make an improvement!

Ask the pupils to record some short snippets of audio about a topic you are currently covering in class and to choose the best of their recordings. Play these together as a class and ask the pupils to constructively comment with suggestions on how to improve the presentation and quality of the recording.

Class activities: Taking in the ambiance

Explore the website **soundaroundyou.com** to explore soundscapes, both near and far. Emulate the site by creating your own sound map using Google Maps via **bit.ly/ pricomp026**. Ask the pupils to use a range of devices as before to record ambient sounds around the school, and hopefully around the local community as a local trip or homework project. Ensure the pupils make an accurate note of where the sound was recorded. Once the sounds have been collected, you can upload them to **audioboom.com** to generate an online link and then plot them on the map in Google Maps.

Plenary

Ask the pupils to record an 'on location' snippet where they use the skills they learned in the class activity to record themselves giving a newsreader-style report about the location they are in, as well as capturing ambient sounds in the background. Choosing a suitable location could be quite a challenge. If this is an issue, cheat! Play a suitable YouTube or other video or audio in the background to give the desired effect. You can then edit the short recordings together into a 'show' to share on a blog, website, via email and/or in assembly.

Useful links

bit.ly/pricomp027 Visual history of audio devices.

Stage 2 Sounds better

Capturing a great recording is tricky and most of us will need a little editing to sound anywhere near the professionals. The basics of editing sound are quite easy to master, but it quickly becomes much more difficult when you try to add in additional effects and features. Television and radio use a combination of recorded sounds from the real world and computer-generated sounds to make a compelling experience for the listener. In this stage, the pupils will explore some of these methods.

You will need
- Devices and software to record and edit audio:
  - Audacity for Windows and Mac **audacityteam.org/download**
  - GarageBand for iPad **bit.ly/pricomp028**
  - RØDE Rec for iPad **bit.ly/pricomp029**
  - PocketBand for Android **bit.ly/pricomp030**
  - Walk Band music studio for Android **bit.ly/pricomp031**
- Music maker websites and apps **bit.ly/pricomp032**
- BallDroppings via web browser **balldroppings.com/js**
- Isle of Tune website and app **isleoftune.com**
- Soundtrap via web browser **soundtrap.com**
- Foley Artistry video **bit.ly/pricomp033**
- Clapperboard (optional) or woodblock/hand clap
- Director's chair (optional)

Getting started
There are a huge number of websites and apps that allow you to make music. Explore some of the ones listed at **bit.ly/pricomp032**. Here are just a few:
- *BallDroppings* – a very easy introduction to creating digital music. Just draw lines and let the balls reverberate to create mesmerising percussive music.
- *Isle of Tune* – shows once again that there are many ways to create digital music. This website and app composes tunes as you build a map of a town. As a car passes an object in the town, it plays a note or sound. Build up a street to create a tune.
- *SoundTrap* – a superb online music suite where you can play and record virtual musical instruments, add a vocal track and upload audio files. It is a big step up from the previous two websites, and a level of musical skill is useful if you wish to create a cohesive piece of music. Build up multiple tracks to produce some complex pieces of music. You can download your creations or share them online.

Class activities: Foley artistry
As any avid listener to *The Archers* will tell you, they don't really record it in Ambridge. They don't even have real cows in the studio. It is the job of a Foley Artist to add those sounds to the recording. See the Foley Artist video at **bit.ly/pricomp033** for some background to the practice.

Find a suitable video clip, approximately 30 seconds in length, to try the technique out. Turn down the volume on the clip and ask the pupils to re-engineer the soundtrack in small groups using musical instruments, vocalisations including the dialogue, or other materials they can find around the classroom. Give the pupils some time to do some research and possibly also some time to gather suitable materials from home as a homework task.

Once the sequence of sound has been planned out, record each of the sound effects in turn using a clapperboard (or hand clap/wood block) to define the start time of the video to make audio editing easier later. This will allow the children to line up the sounds correctly with time 0.00 on the video.

Class activities: Making tracks

Now that you have your audio tracks, it is time to put them all together. Instruct the pupils to use Audacity, or an alternative from the *You will need* list on the previous page, to edit the audio. Audacity is a huge audio editing package with lots of complex functionality. Despite this, it is still the best option to use with this age group and the basic cutting and syncing is fairly straightforward.

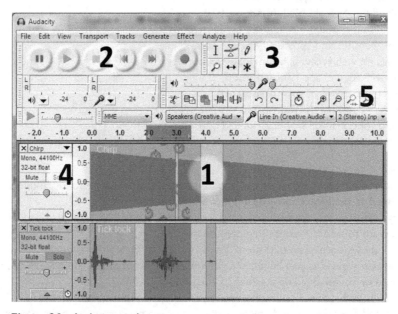

Figure 2A: Audacity windows

The five features of the Audacity window shown above are:
1. Editing area
2. The *Play, Record, Stop* and *Seek* buttons
3. Editing tools – the *Time shift* tool (↔) and the *Section* tool (I) are the most useful
4. The *Mute* function to isolate individual tracks/sounds
5. The *Zoom* tools will allow you to look at your tracks at different magnifications.

Ask the pupils to add their tracks by dragging them from their folder into the editing area. The track will appear as wiggly lines. Find the clapper sound for each track and drag this into a line which shows the time when the video began to play. Drag the soundtrack using the *Time shift tool*, which looks like ↔ and is located near the record button. Listen to the resulting sounds while watching the video again each time a track is added and tweaking where necessary. Export the resulting audio as an mp3 file to your computer (*File > Export*).

Plenary

Take the mp3 file you exported and drag it into a new empty Audacity editor screen. The multiple tracks will now be just one combined track. Ask the children to create a suitable music track for the video to accompany the combined dialogue and Foley track. They can either use real instruments, or they can use digital music makers. Record and drag the audio files into the editing area as before and export the final track.

Try embedding the stimulus video along with the audio your pupils have created into a blog post to show the world.

Stage 3 Hear ye, hear ye

Radio shows need an audience. Broadcasting was once the preserve of a few big corporations. Now, because of advances in technology, anyone can make their voices heard across the globe. In this stage, your class will broadcast themselves to the world. I hope the world is ready!

You will need
- Devices and software able to record and edit audio, e.g. Audacity **audacityteam.org/ download**
- Radio news jingles **bit.ly/pricomp034**
- Creative Commons sounds **freesound.org**
- Creative Commons music **bit.ly/pricomp035**
- Mixlr **mixlr.com** (optional)
- Podbean **podbean.com** (optional)
- SoundCloud **soundcloud.com** (optional)
- AudioBoom **audioboom.com** (optional)
- FM transmitter (optional)

Getting started

Just a Minute is a long-running Radio 4 panel game show where players must speak on a subject for a minute without hesitation, deviation or repetition – it is fiendishly difficult. I have played it using all those rules with Years 5 and 6, but if you drop the repetition rule it becomes much easier for younger children and it is excellent practice for their radio presenter skills. Give the pupils a topic on which they will have lots to say, and pit them against three other players in front of the class. Once they have an understanding of the game, they can move into groups with one person being the arbiter.

Class activities: Musical accompaniment

Explain to the pupils that they are going to create and record a short radio show. Ask your class to record possible title music and jingles to go between each segment. Listen to this radio jingles compilation **bit.ly/pricomp034** for as long as you can stand, and ask your pupils to identify common features. Some key features are a memorable tune and/or slogan, a clear and concise message and objective, and sometimes even a short storyline. Allow adequate time for the class to discuss and give examples of jingles currently on television or radio. Working in small groups, give your class time and the musical resources to create a suitable jingle. Listen to the work in progress and prompt them in the right direction if needed. Once complete, ask the pupils to perform their piece for the class before recording it using the skills they have previously learnt.

Class activities: The show must go on

From the previous stages, your pupils will now have the skills to be able produce the material for a short radio broadcast or podcast. Now they need to explore ways to get their show on the air. As a teacher, there a few options open to you:

• You can pre-record the show and broadcast or publish it later
• You can publish it to the web, or you can broadcast it locally.

Allow the children to publish or broadcast their individual section of audio so they have the experience and know-how to do so, as not everyone will be able to physically broadcast the compiled final show.

Ask the children to plan and prepare for recording a minute-long segment on the show. Relate this to something you are learning about in the wider curriculum. Use the same process of recording as we have covered before (page 33), including background effects and music. Explore websites like **freesound.org** and **bit.ly/pricomp035** – they contain a wealth of excellent audio material to use.

In addition, the pupils can begin to incorporate effects from the *Effects* menu in their audio editing software (e.g. Audacity), such as *Fade in/out*, but using the *Selection tool* to highlight the section for which they wish to use the effect.

To live broadcast locally, you can simply use microphones and any audio sound system your school might have. If the show is pre-recorded, the pupils can connect up a computer or mp3 player to a set of speakers. Alternatively, you can connect your computer/player to a short distance FM radio transmitter, which can be purchased for under 15 pounds from supermarkets and online retailers and will allow you to broadcast to normal analogue radios up to 100 metres away. Your class can set the frequency then begin broadcasting their shows to radios across the school.

Publishing to the web offers a wider audience. You can live broadcast using Mixlr, or uploading to Podbean, SoundCloud or AudioBoom allows you to share the audio via a link or embed on a website or blog.

Plenary

Ask your pupils to gather feedback from their local audience by recording audio interviews, which can be edited and added to the website alongside the original radio show.

Progression

Your pupils have learnt about recording devices and audio editing techniques, recorded dialogue, music and ambient sounds, and tried Foley artistry and audio publishing. They have used a range of devices and software and they have had many things to organise, plan, write and perform.

Cross-curricular links

Depending on the subject matter you decide upon for your show, the possibilities for cross-curricular links are very wide. Performance skills, drama, music and writing will all have been employed to complete the project, and the pupils have learnt many science concepts about sound and sound waves along the way.

Year 2 e-Savvy

Focus: Calling and cyberbullying

What do I need to know?

Communication continues to change at an ever-increasing rate. Today, people are making fewer and fewer phone calls, yet this method of communication will still be with us for a while yet, as the voice conveys information rapidly and intonation provides context and meaning that isn't readily apparent in written forms of communication. Yet it is rare that children are taught to be savvy telephone users.

The National Curriculum for England states that pupils in KS1 should:

- *Use technology safely and respectfully, keeping personal information private; identify where to go for help and support when they have concerns about content or contact on the internet or other online technologies.*

Stage 1 will address staying safe and being respectful, as well as keeping personal information to oneself. Stage 2 will be the first in a series of encounters with cyberbullying and will address inappropriate comments.

> ### Interesting fact
>
> When Alexander Graham Bell, inventor of the telephone, made the first telephone call on 10 March, 1876, to his assistant, Thomas Watson, his first words were apparently: "Mr. Watson, come here, I want to see you."[3]

Key words

Voice over IP (VoIP): a collective term for services like Skype or FaceTime.

---

3 Source: American Treasury of the Library of Congress, Bell's Lab notebook 1, pages 40–41 (image 22). Retrieved 10 March 2016 from www.loc.gov/exhibits/treasures/trr002.html

Stage 1 Calling the shots

On a recent trip to China, I visited a school that taught useful lessons about how to conduct oneself on the telephone – I have exported it here as it is rarely taught in UK schools. With cold-calling and telemarketing becoming an increasingly common phenomenon, it is important to know how to communicate clearly and to develop a healthy scepticism when talking to a stranger on the telephone.

You will need
- Toy intercom or paper cup telephones
- Real telephones
- Devices able to make VoIP calls
- Volunteers to make and receive calls

Getting started
Firstly, let the rest of the school know what you are planning. Have an alternative means of communication available to you in case someone needs to contact you urgently while your phone line is engaged.

Briefly discuss with the class the many different types of communication that are available today and look at pictures or real examples of older technology, such as a rotary dial telephone or old mobile phones.

Before you begin using the telephone, ask the pupils to role-play in pairs different situations where they may need to make a phone call. They can use 'telephone hands' (holding their hands to their ears as if telephones) or they can use paper cups and string for added realism – these can be decorated with drawings of good telephone etiquette and savvy use. Example scenarios may include:
- Inviting a friend over
- Calling for a doctor
- Telling someone you are lost.

Ask a few pairs to act out their calls for the class. Talk about the correct voice to use in each situation.

Class activities: Who you gonna call?
Some of the following will need to be completed by small groups over time, rather than a whole class.

Send a group of pupils to a telephone somewhere else in the school to practise dialling and making calls with a polite telephone etiquette to a group of pupils in your classroom.

Collude with another member of staff to call the pupils one by one with different problematic scenarios, such as cold-calling. The aim for the pupils answering is to be polite, but not to give out any personal information. Example tricky questions may include:
- 'Am I speaking to the homeowner?'
- 'Is this the right number for [name of school or address]?'
- 'I'm in your area and would like to pop round. Will you be in at 1pm?'

This time, ask the member of staff to be on the receiving end of the phone, taking on different roles as required. Ask the children to dial and speak with the staff member, who will act in a range of guises. Scenarios may include:
- Reporting a bike stolen to the police
- Making an appointment with the vet
- Booking cinema tickets.

Class activities: Working 9 'til 3
Now that your class have grasped the basics, it's time to try this in a real context. Instruct your pupils that they are going to man the telephones in the school office. You should inform the community that this is going to happen in advance via the school newsletter. Allowing the pupils to take over will take some bravery and trust, but in my experience they rise to the occasion and I thoroughly recommend you try this for real. If this is not possible, you can set up the situation where the pupils think they are doing the job, but use an internal line instead with members of staff providing the calls. A member of the office staff should be with them at all times, and you may wish to use a telephone with a loudspeaker option so that the adult can hear what is being said.

So as not to bewilder callers, the children's opening greeting might be something like this:

'This is _____ school. Today pupils are practising telephone skills. How may I help?'

Your school's office staff will have you believe that the phone never stops ringing, but if it is quiet, ask a few members of staff or governors to provide calls for pupils to handle.

Class activities: Ask an expert
There are many experts out there who are willing to talk to schools and pupils, but who cannot physically visit the school. Use this to your advantage.

Choose a theme or topic that you are learning about in the wider curriculum and find a local expert or ask online educators on Twitter for a suitable person that the children could contact via Skype. This could be someone in the community, or a teacher at the local secondary school, for example. The level of expertise doesn't necessarily need to be that high, but it will give the activity an extra dimension. Set a date for the call.

Ask the pupils to think of questions about the topic that they wish to ask. When it is their turn to call, make sure they learn how to start the VoIP app and make the call for themselves.

Plenary
As a final consolidating task, organise a timetable for the pupils to call home to parents using a telephone or a VoIP service to explain what they have been learning about. For parents unable to take part, see if your head teacher will take the calls instead.

Stage 2 Cybersecurity

The web is a reflection of the real world in many ways: there are good people who wish to share, collaborate and be sociable; there are also people who delight in making others feel awful...or worse. There shouldn't be any distinction between bullying and cyberbullying – there won't be in a bully's or a victim's mind. It's all bullying. Technology now means that where there was once sanctuary at home, now you can carry around the unkindness in your pocket wherever you go. Your school should have cyberbullying strategies in place which should be outlined in the school's bullying policy. This should be your first port of call before teaching this lesson. Secondly, talk to your network management and the member of staff responsible for overseeing your e-learning platform to find out if it is possible to see whether bullying is happening via school systems.

You will need
- Unkind computer example, edited if necessary **bit.ly/pricomp036**
- Comic book makers **bit.ly/pricomp037**
- Poster-making software, e.g. **canva.com** or **gravit.io**

Getting started
Discuss with the pupils what makes a good friend. Write suggestions on one side of the whiteboard. Next, ask the pupils to suggest things that can cause barriers to friendship such as unkind words, not sharing and not being welcoming to others. Try to make the point that it is not always clear-cut and friends will make mistakes and have off days, which can make others feel sad, but everyone should try to follow the positive side of the whiteboard in their intentions and outlook.

Class activity: Rude computers
Tell the class that you are going to watch a video about bullying. Ask them to talk about what they perceive as bullying and whether it is different to simply being unkind. Discuss where bullying and unkindness can take place, and prompt the children towards technology as being a vehicle for unkindness. Pretend to try to play a video and begin the presentation at **bit.ly/pricomp036** (download and edit the text if you wish). Interact with what the computer is saying and ask the pupils for suggestions for what to do. Prompt for the three principles of cyberbullying prevention:
- Don't respond
- Gather evidence and don't delete everything
- Seek help straight away, as it may escalate if you wait.

Respond to the computer by calling or pretending to call the computing coordinator or the network management for help, as you would want your pupils to. Drive home the point by taking photos of the screen to evidence it, ensuring that you tell the children what you are doing and why.

Ensure that the pupils understand that no one deserves to be bullied or receive unkindness in any form. Reassure them that they will not get into trouble if they seek help and that they can talk to any member of staff about any issues they experience.

Ask the pupils to design a poster (using poster-making software such as **canva.com** or **gravit.io**), write a short response to the computer, record a radio show about the incident and/or design a comic book (**bit.ly/pricomp037**) to reinforce the themes from this lesson.

Plenary
Breaking the silence about bullying is the hardest step. Showcase the work produced by the pupils and invite parents to view it and hear a short presentation about cyberbullying. Do this firstly so that the parents are in the know, and secondly so that your pupils know that the parents are in the know and can talk about these issues with them. Cyberbullying will be visited again in subsequent years so it would be valuable to collaborate with other classes to make this a yearly event.

Useful links

thinkuknow.co.uk
cyberstreetwise.com

Progression

Your class now understand how to communicate clearly and stay safe when answering and calling using the telephone and VoIP services. The children have also begun the long journey into the world of cyberbully prevention, and know what they should do if they fall victim to bullying, both off- and online. This is a message that we will return to.

Cross-curricular links

Cyberbullying crosses over with citizenship and social/emotional development. The telephone call activities also draw heavily on speaking and listening skills, as well as organisational skills.

Year 2 Coding

Focus: Audio, speech and music

What do I need to know?

There are lots to ways that coding can get your message across. Sound and dialogue is an evocative way to speak directly to the user or player of your program, and there are many different ways in which this can be achieved.

The National Curriculum states that pupils in KS1 should:

- *Understand what algorithms are; how they are implemented as programs on digital devices; and that programs execute by following precise and unambiguous instructions.*
- *Create and debug simple programs.*
- *Use logical reasoning to predict the behaviour of simple programs.*

In Stage 1 we will further our understanding of algorithms as the basis of coding. In Stage 2 we will begin to work with audio and dialogue within Scratch and debug simple programs. In Stage 3 we will use the musical coding suite Sonic Pi to create music and debug tunes to make them better. Every element of the above strands of the National Curriculum will be covered over the three stages.

Interesting fact

One of the leading pioneers of software was Margaret Hamilton in 1960. At the age of 24 she began working at NASA and her coding of the first portable computer inside the lunar module was instrumental in taking humans to the moon. (McMillan, 2015)

Stage 1 Omnidirectional

An algorithm can have repeated sections, or loops, and can flow in many directions. In this stage we will begin to think about code in multidirectional ways with inputs from the user and triggers from other lines of code causing a string of code to take a program down a different path.

You will need
- Decomposition video and guide: 'What is decomposition?' **bit.ly/pricomp038**
- Nursery rhyme flow diagrams
- A group of willing choral coders
- A device able to record and play audio
- A3 paper

Getting started
Talk to the class about how we need to break code down into small tasks for the computer to deal with one after the other. Explain that this is called 'decomposition' and it is vital for 'telling' the computer what to do. Watch the BBC video and guide, 'What is decomposition?' at **bit.ly/pricomp038**.

Class activity: Musical algorithms
Do you think that modern music is not as good as when you were young? Do you describe it as just repetitive noise? Use your age-related insights into youth culture to your advantage to create algorithms. Show the class a simple nursery rhyme such as *Hey diddle diddle*. Ask the pupils to interpret the song and list all of the actions mentioned in it:
- The cat plays the fiddle
- The cow jumps over the moon
- The little dog laughs
- The dish runs away with the spoon.

You now have a simple linear algorithm!

Try the same for *Baa baa black sheep*:
- We ask the sheep, 'Do you have any wool?'
- The sheep says, 'Yes, three bags full.'
- The sheep lists, 'One for the master.'
- The sheep continues, 'One for the dame.'
- The sheep finishes by saying, 'One for the little boy who lives down the lane.'

Ask the pupils to work in groups to make a list of steps for other nursery rhymes with a linear pattern, for example, *Little Bo Peep* or *Humpty Dumpty*. If you are able, set each group a different rhyme to work on. You can help them by providing the text and/or images to help them decide on the steps. Ask the groups to report back to the class on their steps and refine their answers together as a class.

Discuss with the class an example that has an element of repetition, for example *Hickory Dickory Dock*. Ask the pupils to help you extract the steps for a few of the verses and list each step on the board. Prompt the children to think about how the rhyme repeats and ask them for suggestions of how it could be rewritten to show this. Create a flow diagram of the rhyme:

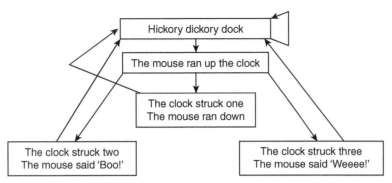

Figure 2B: Flow diagram – *Hickory Dickory Dock*

You can demonstrate how this works by pre-recording yourself or a volunteer chanting each section of this, and then playing them in order from your computer. You will have to make multiple copies of the repeated tracks. You can add a number to the front of the file name to ensure that they play in the right order.

Divide the class into five groups and assign one section of the song, *Hickory Dickory Dock*, for each of them to perform in order. Differentiate or shuffle the sections, as some are easier to do than others.

Ask the pupils to map out their own repeating rhymes. Counting songs/chants allow you to include the idea of a variable, or something with changes. *Five little Speckled Frogs* or *Ten Green Bottles* are good examples.

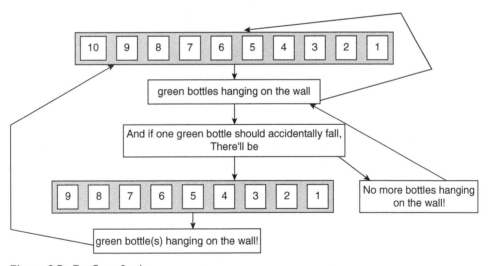

Figure 2C: *Ten Green Bottles*

Plenary

Ask the pupils to research a simple pop song that has repeating lyrics and ask them to map it out on A3 paper. Use the paper to 'conduct' the whole class to sing or chant that song. For the more able, you can ask the pupils to create alternative lines to replace some of the existing lyrics.

Stage 2 Speak out

Computer games are full of sound, talking and dialogue. Today's blockbuster games are more like interactive movies than the basic games we grew up with, and telling the story through sound and stunning visuals is the norm. In the program Scratch, there are three ways to 'say' something or make sounds, and this is what we will explore in this stage.

You will need
- Minecraft speech bubble **bit.ly/pricomp039**
- Devices with microphones able to run Scratch
- Polite fish **bit.ly/pricomp040**

Getting started
Take a look at how audio and speech bubbles are used in popular computer games. For example, see how Minecraft players can both talk in a chat window, and how the game can also be modified to include speech bubbles (see **bit.ly/pricomp039**). Games have their own story arcs, and speech and music are essential to the player's experience. The pupils will learn much more about this in Year 6. Draw on the children's knowledge and ask them to research and suggest examples. Their knowledge will vastly outstrip my feeble examples!

Class activities: Speech bubbles
Instruct the pupils to open Scratch and to locate the *Looks* section of code blocks. At the top of the blocks you will see the following four code blocks:

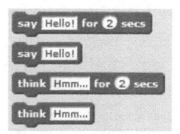

Figure 2D: Dialogue

The first two add speech bubbles to your sprite for an allotted amount of time or until the code instructs it to stop; the second does the same but with thought bubbles:

Figure 2E: Scratch 'say'

Ask your pupils to use a trigger from the *Events* feature and the *wait* string from the *Control* area to create a dialogue between two sprites where only one is speaking at a time. Hint: the dialogue for one sprite will be the same length of time as the wait for the other sprite.

Class activities: Polite fish

The fish at **bit.ly/pricomp039** are a little over-crowded and are getting cranky. The task is to debug the code and add more so that all of the six sprites are polite when they bump into all of the other five. Currently, only the crab is being polite to everyone.

To do this, ask the pupils to make a copy of the project, save it to their account and remix the code. Once the program has been debugged, press save again (*File > Save*) to save the changes to their account.

Tip: You can duplicate code in two ways on Scratch: if you are copying it for the same sprite, right click and press *Duplicate*; if you want to copy from one sprite to another, drag the block to the receiving sprite's square icon at the bottom left of the screen.

Class activities: Noisy sprites

Ask the pupils to add a background and two or three sprites of their choice to the foreground in Scratch. Tell them to add some kind of motion, which isn't too fast, to make them move around the screen.

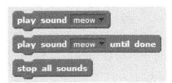

Figure 2F: 'Meow'

Instruct the pupils to open the pink *Sound* code blocks. They will see these three blocks:

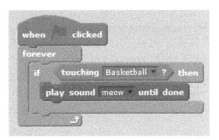

Figure 2G: 'If touching basketball'

Ask them to experiment with these and the other types of code they have already encountered, such as *Motion* code and triggers from the *Events* feature. They should find with these that their sprite will only make the noise once. Add the *Forever* block to make the sound happen each time the conditions are right. Also, ask the pupils to try the *If* and *Touching* blocks commands, which they may have noticed from the polite fish activity.

There is an example of *Noisy sprites* at **bit.ly/pricomp041** and the kind of simple interactions you can make.

Class activities: Recording from scratch

Your pupils may have discovered that the pink *Play sound* block has the option to record a sound in the drop-down box. You can also access more audio options by clicking on the grey *Sounds* tab above the code categories. You will see a window similar to this one:

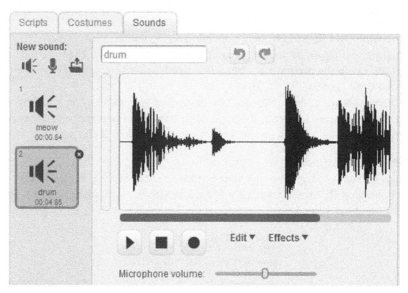

Figure 2H: Recording on Scratch

You will notice the wave form; this is an image of the sound, and can be edited by clicking and dragging across the wave form to select a section. Click on *Edit* for options like *Cut*, *Copy* and *Paste*, or press *Effects* to manipulate the sound.

You also have the ability to add additional sounds to your program. There are three buttons below where it says *New sound*: the left button gives you access to the sound library, the middle button allows you to record using a microphone, and the right button allows you to upload sounds from files on your computer.

Once the sound has been imported into your project, it will appear down the left of the image shown above and you will then be able to access it using the pink *Play sound* block.

Plenary

Ask your class to design a project that uses all three types of speech and audio: speech bubbles; default sprite sounds and those from the library; uploading and recording audio from outside Scratch. Ask pupils to practise using as many different types of code as they can from what they have learnt so far and, if possible, link it to something you are covering in the wider curriculum.

Stage 3 Coding music

Scratch is able to produce programmable digital music with blocks from the bottom half of the *Sound* category. But there is a platform specially designed to create digital music from code that takes this to a whole new level.

You will need
- A device able to run Sonic Pi **sonic-pi.net**
- Headphones for each device to protect your sanity

Getting started
Invite any of your (hopefully) musical children to demonstrate their musical prowess for the class. Ask them about notes and timings, and how these are represented in music notation. Show an example of sheet music to the children and briefly explain how this encodes the music for the musician to read. Explain that they are going to do the same with computing code to tell a computer what to play.

Open Sonic Pi and copy, paste and play the code at **bit.ly/pricomp042**. (You will need a Google account for access but this is free and simple to set up.)

Take your class on a tour around the platform, highlighting the main features (see below). Spend a little time looking at the help area, as this will aid their independent learning later.

Figure 2I: Sonic Pi

The main features are as follows:
1. The code editor window is where the magic happens! This is where you write the code to make music. Under this window you can see buffers. Each buffer page is independent of all

the others, meaning that a change on one buffer page will not change the other pages. You can think of these as separate files which happen to run on the same program, so you can experiment and copy the code between the pages to refine your music.

2. The control buttons are mostly self-explanatory. The three that might not be so obvious are: the *Run* button, which allows you to listen to what your code produces; the *Size* button, which changes the font size of your code; and the *Align* button, which makes sure indents are in the right place (this happens when you run the code anyway).

3. Section 3 is a real time log of what code is playing.

4. The help area is a complete guide to Sonic Pi and contains much more information and advanced settings than I have outlined here. You can copy and paste code from these pages by highlighting the text and right-clicking it into your own code.

Class activities: Basic beeps and repeats

In Sonic Pi there are many different ways to code the pitch of a note. One way is similar to the number of steps in Scratch; your pupils can set the pitch as a number. Ask them to type in:

```
play 80
play 70
play 60
```

You should find that the computer runs all three notes at the same time. Just like in traditional music, pauses and rests are important. This is coded by using the *Sleep* operation. Amend the code to include a sleep for one second after each note.

```
play 80
sleep 1
play 70
sleep 1
play 60
sleep 1
```

Like the *Repeat* or *Forever* block in Scratch, there will be times when you want the code to loop and repeat. Ask your pupils to add the *Times* operation shown below. The number 4 in the code indicates how many times you want this section to repeat. You will also see that there is a coding word: *do*, as in do something, and an *end*. Think of these like the opening and closing of mathematical brackets with everything between them happening, in this case, four times. Just like in maths, these 'brackets' can have other brackets inside them, creating some very complicated patterns.

```
4.times do
    play 80
    sleep 1
    play 70
    sleep 1
    play 60
    sleep 1
end
```

Ask your pupils to experiment with the variables and listen to the results.

Class activities: Sonic instruments and notes
So far the children have been using the default instrument on Sonic Pi. Instruments are called 'synth', short for synthesizer. If you type *use_synth* followed by a space, a list of all the synths should appear as a small scrolling window. Ask your pupils to choose one and then also type the command *play* and a number. It should look like this:

```
use_synth :piano
play 80
```

All the notes that come after the *use_synth* command will use that synth, or instrument sound. So if you choose the piano sound, all the following notes will be piano notes until you choose something else. Ask them to add more notes and some sleeps into the code so it looks similar to the code below. Try adding some decimals to make shorter pauses:

```
use_synth :piano
play 80
sleep 0.5
play 85
sleep 0.5
play 85
sleep 0.5


4.times do
    play 90
    sleep 0.125
end
```

Add in a different synth somewhere in the sequence, e.g.
```
use_synth :piano
play 80
sleep 0.5
play 85
sleep 0.5
play 85
sleep 0.5


4.times do
    use_synth :fm
    play 90
    sleep 0.125
end
```
Your class can change the length of time a note is held in two ways: use the *release* operation, which is similar to the length of time one's finger lingers on the piano key. You can also use the *sustain* code, which has the same function as the sustain pedal on a piano,

in that it controls the length of time it takes for the note to fade away. Ask your children to try both of them in their code:

```
use_synth :piano
    play 80, sustain: 2
    sleep 0.5
    play 85
    sleep 0.5
    play 85, release: 2
    sleep 0.5
```

Also try *amp* to change the volume; try fading in with *attack*, and setting fade-out time using *decay*.

If you are a musician and want to write in standard notes, you can use these in Sonic Pi. Instead of writing the number, write *play*, followed by a colon, followed by the note letter. You can also include flats (b) and sharps (s) and even denote which octave you require by typing a number after the note. Without an octave number this defaults to the 4th octave. Some examples:

E flat in the 3rd octave would be **play :Eb3**
F sharp in the 4th octave would be **play :Fs4** or simply **play Fs**

Let's add some to our code:
```
use_synth :piano
    play :C, sustain: 2
    sleep 0.5
    play :Ds
    sleep 0.5
    play :Ds5, release: 2
    sleep 0.5
```

Class activities: Sampling

The last major component is sampling. Samples are snippets of music and beats of various lengths. They are independent of the current choice of synth, so they are useful as backing tracks, beats and much more. Ask your pupils to open a different, blank buffer page and to type *sample*, followed by a space. They should then see a drop-down list of all the available samples. Ask your class to try adding a variety of samples, synths, notes, sleeps and operations together to see what they come up with.

```
8.times do
    sample :ambi_soft_buzz, amp: 3
    sleep 0.1
    sample :elec_twang
    sleep 0.4
end
```

There are extensive examples of code within the platform. See the examples tab at the bottom in the help window. Ask your pupils to copy and paste elements of the code into their own code to experiment with what happens.

Class activities: What a performance!

So far your class has been doing lots of experimenting and learning how the platform works. Neither the experimenting nor the learning should stop, but it is time to focus on a goal. Ask the pupils to design a class album of pieces for different occasions. They should work in pairs to create a few different pieces, including slow, moving pieces of classical music, some pop music and dance music. The process will take many hours of lessons and, as Sonic Pi is free, the children should be encouraged to work on their code at home, transferring the code to and from school as text documents or via (parental) email.

Plenary

Ask the children to listen to the music and sounds created by their classmates. Ask the children to offer feedback about the music. Ensure that the music code is saved, then ask the children to remix another group's work to see if it can be improved.

Useful links

bit.ly/pricomp043 Raspberry Pi lessons.

Progression

Pupils will have extended their computational thinking and will have begun to see that input can change the behaviour of code and alter its path. They will also have learnt how to communicate with the user of their program and give an immersive experience using text dialogue, audio and music. Your class has also developed the coding skills to produce music via Sonic Pi and furthered their understanding of coding in general as a result.

Cross-curricular links

Music is the obvious link, but as with all coding, there is a lot of maths involved too. The pupils must develop a sense of timing and rhythm to code the music well. There is also an element of English involved through writing speech bubble text.

Year 3 Using and understanding computing

Focus: Communication and networking

What do I need to know?

Establishing an online presence is an increasingly important aspect of modern life and this will only become more so in the future. The web now augments our social life, and it is the main vehicle for business and work. Luckily for my generation, the web wasn't pervasive during our reckless teenage years. Young people today have the added complication that it is the social norm to catalogue one's existence in multimedial detail, and largely in the public arena. If they are not sharing photos of their Friday night adventures on social media, there is an event or experience that a friend is tagging them in. I strongly believe that the advantages of using technology greatly outweigh the negatives, but as educators it is our role to help learners make the right choices to promote the pros and conquer the cons.

The National Curriculum states that pupils in KS2 should:

* *Understand computer networks including the internet; how they can provide multiple services, such as the world wide web; and the opportunities they offer for communication and collaboration.*
* *Select, use and combine a variety of software (including internet services) on a range of digital devices to design and create a range of programs, systems and content that accomplish given goals, including collecting, analysing, evaluating and presenting data and information.*

In this section we will explore publishing to the web, communication and becoming a networked citizen.

Interesting fact

Dunbar's Number, named after evolutionary anthropologist Robin Dunbar, is the approximate number of meaningful relationships an average person has. According to Dunbar, this number seems to hold true on social media as well as offline examples. The number is approximately 150 relationships. (Krotoski, 2010)

Key words

Feed: a list of messages or articles – common feeds include Facebook and Twitter posts and RSS feeds from websites.

Stage 1 Say what?

We've already looked at digital technology as a means of communication. It is not an understatement to say that the Internet, the web and a plethora of apps and software developments have revolutionised the way we communicate. In this section we will introduce your class to a range of communication methods that are popular today.

You will need
- Access to email accounts
- Image of an example inbox **bit.ly/pricomp044**
- Scrap paper
- A large space, preferably outside
- Getty Images **gettyimages.co.uk**
- YouTube **youtube.com**
- Vimeo **vimeo.com**

Getting started
Take your class to a large space, preferably outside. Give each pupil some paper and something to write/draw with. Ask the children to group themselves in pairs and label themselves 'scribes' and 'receivers'. All pairs stand in lines facing each other about two steps apart from their partner, so all scribes are in one line and all receivers are in a parallel line. Quietly, or pictorially, so the receivers cannot see, give a message for the scribes to convey to their partners in any way they can from the set distance. This should be easy enough. Then increase the distance they are apart to five steps, then ten steps – how do they convey the message? Some pupils might think to screw up the paper and throw it, or hold up the paper to show it to their partner. This is good creative thinking – encourage this sort of thing. Increase the distance to 50 metres so that throwing or just holding the paper up may not work; keep increasing the distance and watch the children innovate their way out of the problem. The lesson here is that the greater the distance, the greater your ingenuity must be to communicate over that distance.

Class activities: Email in a bottle
Despite many attempts to reinvent it or replace it altogether, email has been a vital means of communication for the past three decades.

Many schools have an email system for the pupils. If not, you will need to set up some email accounts for this activity.

Show the children the downloadable and editable image of an inbox at **bit.ly/pricomp044**.

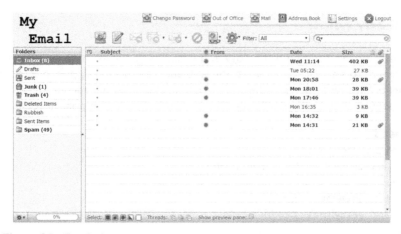

Figure 3A: Email inbox

Add your own safe emails to the inbox from people the children know at school. Talk to the children about the different functions of the features you can see. For example, explain that the messages can be accessed by clicking on the subject title; talk about the folders that can be used to organise messages; and discuss the difference between 'compose', 'reply' and 'forward'.

Teaching how to use an email system can be dull, but creating narrative is just one way to make it more interesting. Adapt the following idea by using your own themes or character(s) to fit in with your curriculum if you can.

Before the start of the lesson, send out a personalised email like this:

From: Stan Ded (StrandedOnIsland@gmail.com)
Subject: Email in a bottle

Dear _____

I know your teacher, _____, and I know that you will be able to help me. I have been stranded on this island with no food rations, but with excellent Wi-Fi, for two weeks. I don't have a bottle to send a message in, so I'm emailing you instead. I need some advice about living and surviving here. I've taken photos of some things I think I can eat, but I would like your opinion.

Can you give me some advice about what I can do for shelter?

Lastly, if you know any tips for training monkeys or taming tigers, please let me know.

Stan

Attach three images to your email, two of some exotic edible fruit and one of something that looks poisonous, like a toadstool or a blue frog.

Ask the pupils to sign in to the email client. If it is the first time they have logged on to their email account, take them on a tour, making sure you show them: the inbox, sent, spam and deleted folders and location of the contacts/address book.

If you have instilled a healthy scepticism in your pupils, they will hopefully think twice about opening an email from a stranger and downloading the attachments. If so, then congratulate them but also reassure them that you do in fact know Stan, and that it is safe to open. If they open it without a second thought, take this opportunity to instil a little scepticism.

Ask the pupils to identify how formal the email is and ask them to pitch at a similar level in their reply.

Tell the pupils to view the attached images and to make their assessment of what Stan should do, and research options for shelter, including an image to attach. They can also include information and advice about training monkeys and safety tips around tigers if they wish.

Ask them to reply to the email using the *Reply* button. Point out how the *Subject* text is copied from the previous email and that *Re:* has been added. Ensure that you show the children how to attach an image for the reply and locate the *Send* button.

Once your class have sent their emails to Stan, send a reply from him, saying something along the lines of:

Hi _____

Many thanks for the advice. It has helped me so much.

I think it is time I left the island and found my way home. Can you find out where the island is and how far away from the UK I have travelled? My GPS says I am at 51.463092, -2.621900.

If I never make it home I just want to thank you for all your help.

Stan

Ask the pupils to research where the island is (using Google Maps) and reply to Stan about his location. The above coordinates are for a small island located at Bristol Zoo Gardens.

Class activities: To me... to you

Ask the pupils to form writing groups of five to six people, with each member of the group working on a separate device. Send out around eight story openings or stimuli, and encourage the children to compose a follow-on story of their own, where each child in turn adds to the existing story by writing a further sentence. Each member of the group adds a sentence to one of the short stories then presses *Forward* to send everything written so far to the next person in the group. If a peer spots an English error in a previous entry, they should be allowed to fix it. As *Forward* is pressed, the system should add the email address of the writer, so you will be able to track who wrote what for assessment purposes.

Plenary

Ask the class to take charge of (non-essential) email communications to their parents for the whole week. Ensure that the parents are made aware of this beforehand and make sure that both the pupils and adults are aware that the emails will not be corrected by the teacher before they are sent – stick to this! Provide support if the children ask for it, but it is important to their independence that they initiate this and check their own text thoroughly.

Stage 2 Getting connected

Over the last decade, social media has become pervasive and has changed the way we gather information and interact. Most social networks have a lower age limit of 13 years old but it is naive to think that this will stop pupils signing up anyway, and it is beneficial to teach them how to use social networking sites responsibly in a controlled space before they choose to try it without experience. The popularity of different social networks rises and falls in a matter of years. Do your research into what is currently in vogue with teens and explore that platform yourself so you can relate what you are doing in class to what they are probably doing at home. When I asked my own Year 5/6 class about what they use, half of them were on Facebook, a third used SnapChat and many had their own account on WhatsApp.

You will need
- Devices able to access **twiducate.com**
- Sticky notes

Getting started
Discuss how your class communicate with each other outside of school. List all the answers on sticky notes and place them on the board. Ask the pupils to discuss the features of each means of communication and, as a class, try to group them into similar methods. Ask the pupils to think of the pros and cons of each category.

Class activity: Getting social
Twiducate is a closed social network designed especially for schools to teach children how to use networks responsibly, and it is based on Twitter. The platform consists of a text box, similar to an email textbox, with various formatting options such as bold, underline, alignment and many more. You can also add links and images to the posts.

> *Important: grant access to another member of staff so the feed is visible by another adult for your own protection if needed. Also, I would recommend you disable the chat function and the ability for pupils to delete posts by changing the settings in the* Profile *area.*

Before the lesson, you will need to add your pupils to the platform via the *Students* tab. Show the class the platform and demonstrate some of its functionality.

Just like a normal social networking site, the pupils can edit their profile. Even though this is a closed platform, ask the children to treat it as if it were open and tell them to complete their profiles accordingly.

Ask the class to attempt a few posts to try it out; include a few posts with images. Most of social media is based on live events. Simulate this with a video based on a topic you are covering in the wider curriculum. Ask your pupils to write live updates about what is happening, using the device's camera to take photos to post if they are able.

Plenary
Once the pupils have the right idea it can be a permanent fixture in their learning routine to give you continual feedback about their learning and to provide a superb plenary.

As your pupils are not allowed to post directly to Twitter themselves, you can also use Twiducate to take suggestions from your class about things to post to your class Twitter feed by asking them to tag their posts with *#Twitter* if they think it might be suitable.

Networking for teachers

Social networking is simply the best tool for professional development, with Twitter being at its core. Bar none – every teacher should be on Twitter. Nowhere else can you can access the ideas and resources of thousands of educators, discuss classroom practice with experts and front-line educators and keep informed about policy updates and educational news. It will enable you to tailor your professional development to your needs like no meeting, course, INSET or professional review. It is a resource you cannot ignore, and in time, do without. Twitter is also a great way to keep the school community informed and engaged.

Signing up to Twitter is simple. You just need an email address and an idea for a *handle* or username that the community will know you by. To talk to another user you simply write an @ in front of their handle. Twitter's micro blogging posts can only be a maximum of 140 characters long so you are able to browse a lot of information in a very short space of time. You can also add images, short videos and links to tweets, so they are often used to signpost to more in-depth content. You *follow* interesting people and organisations so you see their updates in your timeline. For example, search for *@UKEdChat* and *@UKEdMag* for open-access news, articles and resources for UK educators.

Users can share posts they want their followers to see by pressing the *Retweet* button and you can save interesting posts by pressing *Like*. To find topics you are interested in or to read and join discussions, just search for labels called *hashtags* or include it in your post if you want others to find it. The *#UKEdChat* hashtag is the main hub for UK educators on Twitter.

Social media can be a procrastination tool for many, but if used professionally to find ideas, collaborate with others and improve your knowledge and classroom practice, it is like the biggest and best staffroom you could ever wish for and you will get so much more than you put in. Find me on Twitter at *@ICTmagic* and I will do my best to guide you through it.

Stage 3 Clever blogs

An audience can bring so much to a performance. Whilst I'm sure you enjoy seeing the improvements in your pupils' work and that they benefit from your enthusiasm and guidance, there is much to be gained by producing work that will be seen by non-teacher eyes, and beyond its twice-yearly showing at parents' evening.

Blogging is an ideal way to use technology to improve both the quality of writing and other skills, and give your class an audience to support and cheer on their learning.

You will need
- Devices that can access blogging platforms, such as **wordpress.com** or **blogger.com** (you will need a Google account to access Blogger, but this is free and simple to set up)
- Getty images **gettyimages.co.uk**

Getting started
Before introducing blogging to your class you will need to set up your own blogging site. For this brief tutorial, I will guide you through setting up Wordpress as my blogging platform of choice, but there are many other sites that work in a similar way and most are free.

Firstly, go to **wordpress.com/start**. You will be prompted to choose a 'theme' to set the design of your blog. This will need some consideration, as this will ultimately affect how readers interact with the blog. You can change the theme later, so your choice doesn't need to be permanent.

Next, you will need to choose a domain, or the address of the site. A short name of your school and the class name is a safe choice, but it needs to be easy to find and to remember for both the children and their expectant audience. Then you choose a plan and create your login details.

Next, you will need to provide the children with login details. Go to the *My Site* dashboard and click *Add* on the *People* tab. You will need to send out email invites to allow your pupils to link to the site. If you have access to your pupils' email login details, I would suggest you set up the accounts yourself so you can be sure it is done correctly and so you can make a record of their blog login details. This will take some time, but it is beneficial. Lastly, when you set up the pupils' accounts, set their role to *Contributor*. This will allow you to vet and correct any post before it goes live for the public to read.

The possibilities for how to use your blog are infinite. Below are just a few of my favourite suggestions.

Class activities: Author connections
Show the children a pre-made blog you have written about setting up the blog and some of the uses you hope you get out of it, but write this as a third-person narrative. Tell the children that they will 'complete the story' of how the blog adventure will unfold.

Instruct the class to log in to the blog site and to click the *New post* button. Take the pupils on a quick tour of the blog post composer, which is similar to the email platform and Twiducate that they have met recently. The big difference is that they have a *Submit/ Publish* button instead of a *Send* button. Show them the two tabs: *Visual* and *HTML*. The *Visual* tab allows the user to edit the text and images in a similar way to an email. The *HTML* tab allows you to add and edit HTML code to embed media easily into your blog.

Ask the pupils to go to **gettyimages.co.uk** and to choose an image to embed. Once they find their image, ask them to press the *Embed* button. This will bring up a preview, size options and the HTML code for your pupils to copy and paste into the HTML tab. Because the image is not directly stored on the blog, but still resides on the originator's site, some organisations like Getty do allow you to use their images freely as embedded media.

Next, ask the class to search YouTube or Vimeo for a tasteful video to also embed. Press the *Share* button and repeat the copying and pasting of code into the HTML tab.

Their writing task is to write a chronological description of the video using the knowledge and skills they have already developed about using the blogging platform. You can make the description as simple or as detailed as you wish.

Class activities: Guest blogs
There are so many interesting people from history or fiction to whom it would be wonderful to talk. Luckily, your class have that ability through their blog, and this can be a great stimulus for non-blogging activities too. As part of their work on biographies and autobiographies, instruct the class to create a piece of writing about a historic figure or their own fictitious famous person. Model this by creating your own to show them. Use embedded images and other media in your example and encourage them to do the same in their own post later.

Once the pupils are signed in, ask them to add questions to your character's blog entry via blog comments, and either answer these while the pupils are working, or ask an accomplice to answer as many of these as possible as they are being asked.

Ask the pupils to write a similar blog entry about a historical or fictional character they know about or can research about. This should include embedded media to support their blog post. Ensure that the children know how to submit their finished blog and encourage them to read each other's blogs and add questions, which the author can follow up in character.

Class activities: Beyond the sea

Blogging as a class or a whole school is a wonderful way to share what is happening in schools, but the experience of connecting with classes and children in other schools and in other countries takes this to a whole new level. Naturally, you need to find suitable classes to team up with. Social media is a superb way to ask if anyone is interested in joining the project, and there is an international map of educators on Twitter at **bit.ly/pricomp045** which might be a useful starting place for approaching others. As an example, a few years ago I set up a project at **speechbubbles.wikispaces.com** with the goal of teaching English to Chinese children and Mandarin to UK pupils. Grouping two to four classes works well, as it creates enough content to be interesting, but not unwieldy. You can invite guests to join your blog as contributors, copy your partner's posts directly into your blog, or set up an independent blog for the project. Sharing cultural and local life is fascinating and it is intriguing to see how schools differ between countries.

Plenary

Whilst a large number of view counts is not the main focus of a class blog, it certainly is nice to see those numbers rise. Ask the children to write a blog post that they feel will be popular, tailored to their audience and widely read, and ask them to promote their own writing with their new email and social media skills and see whose post gets the most reads after a week. Each child could compose the text for a promotional media tweet on the class or school Twitter feed to go beyond the school.

Useful links

quadblogging.com QuadBlogging

Progression

During this section, your children have moved from being passive digital consumers to global digital citizens publishing their thoughts and ideas to the web. They are now communicating via email to individuals and they have begun publishing to the masses online via social media and blogs. However, the true progression will be seen in their continual use of these tools to further their learning. Introducing blogging in Year 3, at the start of KS2, should be a deliberate move to start something that will carry through the rest of their primary education.

Cross-curricular links

The cross-curricular links are unidirectional and vast. There is the potential to publish every type of English writing or any other text for any subject to a real audience. The children can publish media to their blogs, making it the perfect consolidation tool for most subjects and writing – they can make videos or audio files, and create images to post, which are wonderful ways to reflect on their learning.

Year 3 e-Savvy

What do I need to know?

The web is not analogous to the publishing world with a few gatekeeper organisations filtering what we see, as is so often thought. It is more like the street corner where anyone with a belief or motivation can shout about what they like for all who are passing through to hear. This has both positive and negative consequences. It means that in countries with largely unfiltered and unmonitored access, it is a powerful force for democracy where anyone can make themselves heard. However, there are no checks and balances to ensure the information isn't misleading, biased, flatly untrue, or wilfully mischievous or malicious. The onus is completely on the readers to make that judgement for themselves, and often with little evidence to back this up either way. The number of sites with a particular assertion is no guarantee to the validity of a claim either, and we live in a world where urban myth, pseudoscience and rumours are allowed to pass unchallenged by the majority of the population. There are no easy answers to this as an individual web user, other than to have a healthy scepticism of everything you see on the web and to check the validity of the source yourself. This section is designed to develop that scepticism and to improve the pupils' skills at checking information.

The National Curriculum states that pupils in KS2 should:

* *Use technology safely, respectfully and responsibly; recognise acceptable/unacceptable behaviour; identify a range of ways to report concerns about content and contact.*
* *Use search technologies effectively, appreciate how results are selected and ranked, and be discerning in evaluating digital content.*

This section will address the second strand about helping the pupils to develop an understanding of trusted sources and an understanding of the soapbox culture of the web.

Interesting fact

Precise estimates vary, but as of 2016 there are approximately one billion live websites, but only about a quarter of those are active, with the average life of a website being around 100 days. (**internetlivestats.com** and Lafrance, 2015)

Stage 1 Checking the facts

There are many websites that I like, but I love a good educational spoof. There are websites that have been designed for educational purposes to intentionally mislead young users so that they learn a valuable lesson in checking facts.

You will need
- Devices that can access the following spoof sites:
  - **allaboutexplorers.com**
  - 'Help save the endangered Pacific Northwest Tree Octopus from extinction' **zapatopi. net/treeoctopus**
  - 'Free forever dog island' **thedogisland.com**
  - 'Boilerplate – mechanical marvel of the nineteenth century' **bit.ly/pricomp046**
- Access to **theonion.com**

Getting started
Tell the pupils that they are going to conduct some research about one or more of the topics from the websites above – try to fit them into your current topic if you can. Ask the children if they know any information about the selected topic already. You will be amazed at what information they already know about a non-existent topic!

Class activities: Factual fibs
Tell the pupils that you want them to collect 'good' information and then write or blog a factual piece about the topic. Also ask them to check the information with other sources – which they will fail to do. Once the pupils have completed their writing, reveal that the websites are inaccurate and mostly made-up. Ask the children to revisit their writing to attempt to select any information that might be true. Next, tell your class to add more made-up but seemingly plausible information to their writing.

Class activities: Misspent youth
Naturally, you intend to write your memoirs one day, so why not ask your pupils to help you write about your hazy younger years now! If you are feeling brave and thick-skinned, ask the pupils to write a biography of your school days; otherwise use a character from fiction. You can even provide them with a few pieces of evidence, such as photos, newspaper cuttings, etc. – all of which can be completely unreal. Impose two criteria on their writing: firstly it must be completely made-up; secondly it needs to be plausible. Once complete, choose a selection of pupils to read out their work, and ask the rest of the class to challenge any implausible information and explain their reasoning. If you wish, you can ask the pupils to revise their work from the feedback from the inquisition.

Class activities: Unbelievable believability
Instruct the pupils to use the school library and their own knowledge to write or blog a piece of almost completely accurate factual information – except that within this accurate information, they have to try to sneak three untruths past the reader. Each child should choose a different topic, as researching the same topic would give an advantage to those

guessing the untruths. Ask the class to ensure that the untruths are substantial, stand-alone facts. Once complete, the pupils can swap their text and make their guesses.

Plenary
Show the pupils a variety of news stories from websites and ask them to assign their believability rating from one to ten. The Onion at **theonion.com** is an interesting source of funny and made-up news for this, although choose wisely as the site does have some adult content. Once the pupils have rated the article, discuss their reasoning and what clues they used. Finally, reveal which articles are factual and which are not.

Useful links

clonezone.link Adapt text and images on websites.
goggles.mozilla.org Use code to change text and images on websites.

Stage 2 Finding the source

Cross-referencing and checking what you find online is a vital skill in today's opinion-driven, photoshopped world. In this stage, we will continue to make the pupils discerning researchers in an attempt to find the truth in a web of misinformation.

You will need
- Devices able to access the web
- Access to the QI website **bit.ly/pricomp047**
- A few willing members of staff to act out the part of witnesses

Getting started
Discuss with the pupils where they go and who they trust to state correct information. Hopefully you will be high on their list. Ask them to explain their reasoning. Dig further and ask whether it matters what topic the information is about. Would they ask their trusted source for information (if at all) about:
- Sport
- Science
- Technology and gaming
- Fashion?

Class activities: Triple-check
Gather around five to ten facts from the QI website **bit.ly/pricomp047**. Include a source reference and rephrase the facts slightly so they do not appear as the first search result when pupils look them up online. Add some of your own facts to mix in – some of these should be nearly true but are in fact false. Instruct the pupils to use a search engine to try to corroborate all of the facts. Ask them to think about which facts they think are correct and which are false, and to copy and paste links to three supporting websites into a text document.

At the end of the session, tally up the number of websites the children found to confirm the claim and ask collectively which they think are correct. Reveal which facts were correct and discuss any errors, what clues the websites give that they are reliable and what elements shook their confidence. This is likely to be quite difficult.

Introduce the idea of gatekeepers – organisations that have built up the trust of many people and who usually check their sources carefully. The big news organisations and broadcasters are good examples.

Class activities: Witness

Tell the class that they are going to write or blog a police report, which must be completely accurate in every way (spelling and punctuation would be nice, too!). Base the news story on something familiar, like nursery rhymes or childhood fantasy characters, such as the theft of a tooth by the tooth fairy, vandalism by the big bad wolf, or, if it is around Easter time, chocolate eggs going missing from the classroom with large bunny footprints left behind as evidence.

Ask a few members of staff to act in the role of witnesses, one of whom was the person who did the crime. Each witness makes a statement and then the pupils get to ask a few questions each. The pupils should make notes as the information is being given. Once the class have finished their writing, ask them to cross-check and refute their peers' reports either verbally or via blog comments.

Plenary

Direct the children to a webpage for a local newspaper story and ask them to corroborate it by finding out as much about the contextual information (locations, timing, people involved, etc.) as they can. Ask them to copy the text for any element for which they find an additional online reference into a list. Look to see what kind of facts are available online and discuss other ways journalists have to discover and check facts.

Useful links

bit.ly/pricomp048 Conspiracy theories.

Progression

The pupils have furthered their understanding of evidence and researching using information from the Web. They have developed their skills in cross-checking and assessing the validity of items published online.

Cross-curricular links

There are many links with the history curriculum, where historical evidence and the validity of sources is a key feature. There are also many links to English, with biographies and factual report writing being just two examples.

Year 3 Coding

Focus: Hacking, debugging and changes

What do I need to know?

Hacking gets a bad press. But the term 'hacking' doesn't just mean that you need to cancel all your credit cards, or that your emails have been read. In technology circles, 'hacking' means adapting and changing something to divert it from how it normally operates, even though this does include the nefarious access to restricted systems and information. In this section, the little hackers in your class are going to alter some code on web pages to adapt it with their own content. They are going to learn that coding involves problem-solving to fix problems and make the program run smoothly. They are also going to learn how to make changes within their coding projects to transition between characters and places.

The National Curriculum states that pupils in KS2 should:

* *Design, write and debug programs that accomplish specific goals, including controlling or simulating physical systems; solve problems by decomposing them into smaller parts.*
* *Use sequence, selection and repetition in programs; work with variables and various forms of input and output.*
* *Use logical reasoning to explain how some simple algorithms work and to detect and correct errors in algorithms and programs.*

This section will cover all of these strands, with a particular focus on the debugging and correcting errors of bullet points one and three.

> ## Interesting fact
>
> Finding bugs in computer systems can be a very profitable line of work. Companies pay hundreds of thousands of pounds in *bug bounties* each year to members of the public who report flaws in their systems. (Ward, 2014)

Key words

Hacking: adapting and changing something to divert it from how it normally operates.
Debugging: finding coding faults and fixing or improving programming.

Stage 1 Hacking

Incremental change is how most innovation happens and, to quote Sir Isaac Newton, we all 'stand on the shoulders of giants'. Changing, adapting and learning from other people's code is fundamental to learning coding. There isn't a big textbook containing all the possibilities and functions that coding has as it interacts with other algorithms. Coding is as much about tinkering and experimenting as it is about tutorials. So teach your pupils what you know and then don't be surprised if they quickly supersede you. In this stage we are looking at HTML code on websites and tweaking it to see what changes can be made.

You will need
- Devices that can access and use the X-ray Goggles editing tool **https://webmaker.org/ goggles**
- BBC Newsround website **www.bbc.co.uk/newsround**
- Access to the Creative Commons images at **pixabay.com**

Getting started
Edit the BBC Newsround website using the X-ray Goggles editing tool so that one of the headlines and pictures has been changed to some news related to your school, such as 'True content of school's shepherd's pie discovered' or 'Heroic teacher escapes after being trapped under avalanche of unmarked books'. Spin the story out a little to your pupils, and then reveal that you have hacked a copy of the website and later they will be doing the same.

Ask the pupils what they understand as hacking. Talk briefly about the hacker and maker culture of repurposing technology (See 'Making the difference', Burrett, 2015).

Class activity: Hacks and tinkering
Go to the BBC Newsround website and set up the X-ray Goggles toolbar widget so the pupils know how to do the same on their computer later. Start the goggles and click on a headline so the HTML code appears. Demonstrate changing the headline to something like 'Class hacks website' and change the image to the image **bit.ly/pricomp049**.

Repeat the example a few more times so the pupils understand how to do it. Ask the children to set up the X-ray Goggles toolbar themselves and engage it on the BBC Newsround site. Instruct the pupils to copy the method you taught them to change the text and images using licence-free Creative Commons images from **pixabay.com**.

Once the pupils have experimented and practised, ask them to produce a news page on their blog based on recent news and learning. Depending on how your blog has been set up, you may need to remind them that these pages are on the public Web, and they need to include no personal information.

Plenary
Publish a link to the edited pages on the class blog and ask the pupils to comment on the edits. Ask the pupils to choose a website of their choice and repeat the activity. Introduce the idea of remixing programs from Scratch and other platforms to tweak other coders' work.

Useful links

codecademy.com/learn/web Codecademy HTML and CSS.
w3schools.com/html HTML tutorials.

Stage 2 Debugging

The ability to problem-solve is a key skill when coding, and finding solutions often takes a lot of patience and experimentation. In this stage, your class will be confronted with lots of faults and errors to fix and solve.

You will need
- Devices that can access **play.codekingdoms.com**
- Example Scratch debugging game, *Angry fish (debug)* **bit.ly/pricomp050**
- Debugging videos and guide: 'What is debugging?' **bit.ly/pricomp051**

Getting started
'Code kingdoms' is a wonderful site that teaches Java Script programming language by giving the user a range of problem-solving activities to solve, in a child-friendly adventure game environment. With your class, follow the on-screen tutorial and solve the missions until you feel the pupils have understood the basics. You can sign up to an account and return to the site later if you choose.

Class activities: Fishing for bugs
Firstly, show the video and guide, 'What is debugging?' at **bit.ly/pricomp051**.
Begin by talking to the pupils about technical glitches. Ask them to share their experiences of technology going wrong and how it is wonderful when you fix it.

Instruct the children to go to the Scratch debugging game, *Angry fish (debug)* at **bit.ly/pricomp050** and to make a remix copy in their account.

Ask them to search through the scripts carefully to discover the bugs. The 'deliberate' bug is that the strength values are all the same, and so pressing the strength number makes no difference to how the shark moves. Do not limit the pupils to just this, however. If they can genuinely improve the game further, you should let them. Ask the pupils for their feedback about what is wrong with the code and write their suggestion on the board without you confirming or denying whether they are right.

Instruct the class to group themselves in twos or threes and ask them to discuss ways to overcome the bugs for a few minutes. Once they have a plan of action, allow them to set about their task of fixing the bugs individually. Throughout their coding time, showcase how individual pupils have adapted the code, and show what it does on the whiteboard.

Bring their coding time to a close and see what the majority of the children think the 'deliberate' bug was and confirm whether they were right. Talk about other changes they wanted to make to improve the game.

Class activities: Hide bugs and seek
Ask your class to search the Scratch website for a simple game, with not too much code, that they can copy to their account and tweak so it has a few bugs in it. Next, ask them to share the tweaked game link with another member of the class and complete a similar process as in the previous activity, but ask them to write down the process they use on paper. Make sure that they include what they think the bug is and what they attempt in order to fix it.

Once the debugger thinks they have solved the problems they need to team up with the pupil who planted the bug to discuss what they did to fix it and whether it was correct.

Depending on the length of time this takes and the length of the session you have to complete this activity, repeat the process as many times as possible with other children's bugged code.

Class activities: Competitive bug

Ask the pupils to design a completely new game based on the skills they have already learnt. They should complete the game to the best of their ability and save it to their Scratch account. Next, they will make a copy and change just one block of code to mean that the game does not work well. Ask the game designer to write what bug they have added on a piece of paper, to be handed to the teacher with their name on it.

They then swap their project with another pupil. At this point, introduce a competitive element by offering a prize for the first pupil to fix the deliberate bug made by the coder. (It is best to wait until the sabotage has already been made so they will not be tempted to make the bug too difficult to find!) Note that the debugger won't have confirmation that they have fixed the deliberate bug until the end. Once the debugger finishes fixing the fault they think was made they can call time, and you should note down their time, along with the bug they think was the deliberate mistake.

Plenary

Divide the class into 'development teams' of four to five children, and get them working on the games they designed during the last activity with the aim of building and improving each one until it is a finished product. Note that each team will simultaneously be working on four or five projects: each team member tackles one project by themselves and then rotates to another project, which their team mate had been working on. Team up with some of the younger classes to allow the younger children to play the games and give feedback, particularly about any bugs that can be fixed or improved.

Stage 3 Changing, adapting and simulating

Games are rarely static – scenes change, characters move and power-ups cause your sprites to alter; in addition, text, buttons and graphics appear and disappear when instructions are needed, controls are used and additional information is required. In this stage your pupils will explore how to change and adapt the appearance of sprites, background and other items within a game environment.

You will need
- A collection of child-friendly computer games that the pupils have brought in themselves, or use educational games from **bit.ly/pricomp052**
- Devices that can access Scratch **scratch.mit.edu**
- A collection of photos
- A whiteboard and projector
- Twitch **twitch.tv**
- Sleeping Beauty clip **bit.ly/pricomp053**

Getting started
Twitch is a popular video-streaming website where gamers broadcast their game playing live to the Web for others to watch (no, I don't understand why either). Just before the lesson begins, and with the sound muted as this is live, choose a channel of a popular and child-friendly game for the children to view. Ask for a volunteer who knows the game to take the place of the player and to briefly provide commentary.

Either pre-arranged or on a different day, ask the pupils to bring in a few computer games, and source some yourself (or use educational games from **bit.ly/pricomp052**). In pairs, ask your pupils to play and narrate some of the games – record them doing this using a device that can record video. Ask them to repeat the activity, but this time to comment about how the background, characters and other objects change as the game progresses. Once complete, ask them to watch and listen to both videos and explain how the description differs between the two.

Class activities: Walk before you can leap
In Scratch, many of the sprites from the library have a few different versions of the same character in different stances. For example, the default Scratch cat has two positions, which, if run in sequence, give the impression of walking.

Ask the pupils to start Scratch and to choose an *Event* trigger along with the *next costume*, *Wait* and *Motion* settings to make the sprite not just move, but animate its walking. For this they will need to pause using *Wait* between each costume so the change is visible. Once they have the idea, ask them to add a second sprite and to get the two to race across the screen.

Your pupils will find that when the sprites reach the edge of the screen they will just continue going. This can be corrected using the *if on edge, bounce* block from the *Motion* category. However, the sprite will likely turn upside down when they hit the edge and turn around. You can correct this by using the *set rotation style* block from the *Motion* category. Now see if the children can make their sprites walk lengths to and fro across the screen.

Next, ask the children to go to the grey *Costumes* tab and duplicate the same sprite costume, but then use the drawing editor to change it in some way. Once complete, they should then incorporate the new costume into the sequence.

Class activities: Size, hue and layer

Changing the size or colour of a sprite can have many uses in a game. Both functions can be found in the *Looks* category. Change the hue of a value to a specific amount by using the *set colour effect to* block or change by a certain value each time using *change colour effect by*. The latter is useful if you wish to make the sprite flash when it has been hit or gain a special power. Any changes can be reset to the original colours by using *clear graphic effects*. Ask the children to experiment with each of these together with the *wait* block.

Changing the size of a sprite can also be used in many ways, e.g. to signify power-ups with a bigger sprite, or get a sense of perspective as your characters walk into the distance.

Ask the pupils to choose a suitable backdrop to experiment with perspective. Next use the *change size by* and *set size to %* blocks from *Looks*, along with some *Motion* code, to make them appear to slowly disappear into the distance (see Figure 3B).

By default, the last sprite added to a project will be the one that appears in the front layer (just like the layers we met in Year 1, p4), but you may want a different sprite at the front. Challenge your pupils to make two sprites do the waltz. They should flip direction, use costumes, and change their size and layer as they go behind their dance partner, and they can also change colour in a similar way to Sleeping Beauty's dress in the classic cartoon movie (see **bit.ly/pricomp053**). Once complete, showcase some of the pupils' examples on the whiteboard for the class to view.

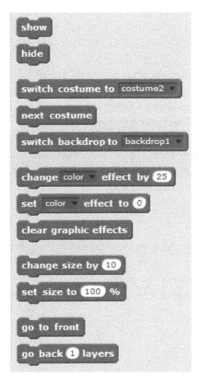

Figure 3B: Scratch costumes

Class activities: Sunrise, sunset

So far we haven't explored backdrop much and it is likely that your children have used a static background. Click on the *Backdrop* window at the bottom left of the screen and add one or two new backdrops from the library, or drawn using the editor; for example, choose a daytime and a night-time scene. Click the grey *Backdrops* tab near the top of the screen and the pupils will see all of the backdrops they have chosen. Delete any you don't need, such as the default blank background.

Go to the *Scripts* tab and add a keyboard trigger, followed by the *switch backdrop to* block. Repeat and select different keys for each of the backdrops in your project.

Next, ask the pupils to use the *wait* block from the *Control* category to automate each scene to last five seconds before moving to the next one.

Tell the pupils that they will be designing a project to present a weather forecast. Ask the children to begin a fresh project and to draw a map as a backdrop. Next, instruct them to duplicate the map many times and to draw a different weather feature on each, ensuring that they keep a blank map in reserve in case they need to duplicate more. Once all the maps have been designed, ask the pupils to set keyboard triggers for each of the different weather types. Add a sprite to the foreground and use speech bubbles from *Looks* to have it deliver the weather forecast.

Class activities: Simulating

Computers and other digital technology have replaced many of the technologies that came before. Coding can be used to simulate many systems, both technological and in the wider world. The following are just two examples of simulations the pupils can try, but many more are possible.

Continuing the weather theme, ask your pupils to design a Scratch project to simulate the weather. They can do this by simply adding a *rain* button that switches the backdrop to a rainy scene, and a *sunny* button that switches the scene to better weather. The pupils can then incorporate this into their weather forecast if they choose.

Coding can also simulate technology. Instruct the pupils to design a simulation of a television and a simple remote control. They can design two channels for the remote control to change between. They could do this with static backdrops, or they could use the *show* and *hide* blocks in *Looks* to make animated sprites that appear and disappear when the button is pressed.

Plenary

Ask the pupils to design a disco scene with simulated flashing lights (set colours), dancers and other sprites chatting and moving at the edge. They can also add basic music using the *Sound* category and their knowledge gained from using Sonic Pi in Year 2 (p49). Once complete, shortlist the best discos and ask the pupils to vote for their favourite.

Useful links

phet.colorado.edu PhET science simulations.

Progression

The pupils have learnt how to adapt code from a website for their own creations. They now know that not all hacking is nefarious and that there are many more meanings of the word than just breaking into websites and computers. The pupils have learnt very important debugging skills, which is a key part of the computing curriculum. They have also furthered their knowledge of coding techniques to change the appearance of sprites and scenes in their projects. Finally, the pupils have looked at simulating systems that can be found in the real world using code.

Cross-curricular links

Debugging is an essential skill in product design, so there are lots of crossovers with the design and technology curriculum. Many English skills were used when editing the news websites, and creating their own news stories is a wonderful stimulus for writing. In the latter stage there were some links with the art curriculum in the use of colour, design and perspective. There was also a link with science in the exploration of simulations – these are a vital feature in much of science, as a way for scientists to be able to test their theories with computer modelling.

Year 4 Using and understanding computing

Focus: Design and collaborative projects

What do I need to know?

The classroom is a wonderfully socially dynamic environment, with thirty or so ideas, opinions, dreams, goals, needs and preferences interacting at any given moment. What a fantastic resource for learning this can be when harnessed. Teachers know the value of collaborating, both between fellow professionals and pupils. Using technology is an ideal method to improve existing collaboration and can offer new possibilities.

The National Curriculum states that pupils in KS2 should:

- *Understand computer networks including the internet; how they can provide multiple services, such as the world wide web; and the opportunities they offer for communication and collaboration.*
- *Select, use and combine a variety of software (including internet services) on a range of digital devices to design and create a range of programs, systems and content that accomplish given goals, including collecting, analysing, evaluating and presenting data and information.*

In this section, we will explore a range of collaborative tools and possibilities, which make working together easier and more productive for both the pupils and you. The pupils will then put these collaborative skills to use to design a range of products.

> ### Interesting fact
>
> The Internet and the Web are not the same thing. The Internet is a collection of interconnected networks, servers and devices. The World Wide Web is a layer of protocols (computer rules) that sit on top of the Internet and this is often accessed via a web browser.

Key words

The Cloud: A generic term meaning storage and services that run completely online without software being stored on your local device. Examples include DropBox, web email and Microsoft's Office Online.

Stage 1 Collaboration

Web-based tools and cloud services now mean that we can access our files and collaborate with anyone from anywhere in the world from most of our web-enabled devices. Indeed, this book was written using a variety of devices in different locations. In this stage, your pupils will learn to use these tools in a range of example activities but the scope of these collaborative platforms can be used much more widely.

You will need
- Devices that can access Google Drive **drive.google.com** (or similar platform)
- Google Apps for Education or other Google accounts
- A whiteboard and projector
- Simple branching story template **bit.ly/pricomp054**
- Three video clips: one fast-paced action clip, one serene video and something else of your choice
- Coggle **coggle.it**
- Flat **flat.io**

Getting started
Tell the pupils that they are going to write a story about ghosts to practise their skills at writing suspense and that they are going to use a new online tool to do it. Introduce Google Drive and the suite of documents, Google Docs, that one is able to make on it. Examine the basic functionality of its text document. Show the children how to: edit the document name at the top left of the screen; change font and font size; align text; carry out basic formatting with bold, italics and underline. Also show your pupils the *My Drive* list.

Class activities: Ghostwriter
Before the lesson, create a simple document for each child with the heading 'Ghostly Tales' or similar, and share the documents via Google Drive with the members of your class. Make sure you have changed the share settings so that anyone with a link to the document can make edits, and before the lesson, collude with other members of staff or trusted older pupils so that they have access to the documents. Ask them to begin making edits and suggestions to the children's documents every now and then during your lesson! The 'ghostwriters' only need make a few changes every few minutes, so it should be feasible for them to monitor a number of documents at once.

Instruct the class to sign in to their Google Drive and begin to write their ghost stories in the document you have set up (see Getting started). Hopefully some of the children will notice the spooky assistants and bring them to your attention. Shrug it off the first few times to allow more children to witness it happening. Once the children's proof is overwhelming, admit that the ghosts have been organised by you but ask them to interact with the ghostwriters as if they were real. Ask the children to use the opportunity to interview the ghostwriters. Make sure the volunteers have a non-gruesome back story that they can share with the children.

Instruct the class to start a new document and talk them through how to share the document via the *Share* button. Ask them to share their document with the next person in the register. Either assign or ask the interviewee to choose the identity of a famous or fictional person, and tell them they will need to conduct some research about that person. The interviewer then types the questions, and the interviewee types the answers (remaining in character!). Ask the pupils to write an interview with the famous person and then write a short biography based on the answers.

Class activities: Collaborative branching stories

Divide the class into pairs and ask each pair to write a short story of 100–200 words using a shared text document in Google Drive on two separate computers at some distance from each other, so that normal means of communication are difficult, so they have to collaborate via the document itself. Once complete, ask the pupils to open a new *Slides* presentation on Google Drive. They should name the presentation, share it between the two contributors and create seven slides using the plus button located near *File* at the top left of the screen. Ask the pupils to break their story up into three logical sections: beginning, middle and end. They should add each section to a different slide by copying and pasting it from the text document.

Next, ask each pair to label their seven slides like the branching story template at **bit.ly/pricomp054**. Ask each pair to collaboratively work on an alternative ending (slide 4) using the same beginning and middle as before. Next, instruct each pair to share their presentation with another pair who should complete an alternative middle section (slide 5) and then complete the final two slides as alternative endings, continuing from their invented slide 5 middle section. Finally, the original writers should return to the presentation and insert hyperlinks, giving the reader choices of which version of the story to follow. They should type some text giving the reader a choice, then insert the hyperlinks by highlighting the choice text and then pressing Ctrl and K to add a link.

Class activities: Quizzes and surveys

Next, use Google Drive to collect data in maths/science, or for pupils to test their fellow pupils' knowledge. Instruct the pupils to begin a new *Form* (*New* > *More* > *Form*) on Google Drive. For example, ask the pupils to set a maths quiz on angles. Tell them to add a title and to enter their questions, including images and videos if necessary. To make things easier later, ask them to design closed questions with a limited number of choices offered to responders, e.g. using multiple choice or check boxes. Ensure that the pupils include a good range of questions, e.g. for the maths quiz on angles, they should include acute, obtuse and reflex angles and other questions.

Once complete, everyone should email the link to their quiz to the rest of the class by pressing the *Send* button. Every member of the class should complete everyone else's maths quiz. Once all the data is in, instruct your pupils to look at the responses to their quiz and to tally (either manually or use the =*SUM(cell:cell)* formula) the number of correct answers and identify where improvement is needed.

Working in small groups of four to six, instruct your pupils to create a new collaborative survey or quiz to practise a particular element of the previous quiz. They should work on the questions in pairs so they can discuss what they will add, sharing it via the *Share* button. Once the quiz is finished, share the link to the live form and ask the class to fill it in. Hopefully the question design will have focused the pupils' understanding on the types of questions that were not answered well the first time around, and you will see an improvement.

Class activities: Mapping tunes

Show the pupils three different short videos with the volume muted. Choose one fast-paced action clip, one serene video and something else of your choice. Start a collaborative mind map on Coggle (**coggle.it**) with the title of each clip as a top-level branch on the map. Invite your pupils to the mind map and ask them to work in pairs on one device to add suggestions for words and phrases to describe the scenes. Show the completed mind map, then discuss and summarise the points that the pupils have raised.

Set up six device stations around the classroom, two for each video clip. Introduce the **flat.io** website: this is a collaborative tool that allows multiple users on separate devices to create and edit music in real time. Ask pairs of pupils to work at each computer for ten minutes at a time before swapping with another pair. Tell the pupils that they will be working on a collaborative atmospheric music score for each of the clips. There will be two groups for each music score, so the pupils will need to organise, plan and improve the piece of music over the two devices. Once the ten minutes are up they will need to take the new pairing through a handover. Continue to repeat the process until the music has been refined and completed. Ensure that all pupils attempt each of the three pieces of music.

Plenary

Ask the pupils to contribute to a new blog post describing their experience of working on a collaborative document. The collaborative blog document can be copied and pasted to the usual blog site once it is complete. Remind the pupils to reflect on the benefits of working together and the disadvantages of real-time collaboration. They should also include possible solutions and give examples of situations where real-time tools are beneficial and when something else is needed.

Useful links

realtimeboard.com Realtime Board.

Stage 2 Building sites

Websites are how most of us interact with the digital world and they have evolved greatly over the years. In this stage, your class will research what makes a good website and begin to design their own.

You will need
- Devices able to access Google Sites **sites.google.com**, and a free Google account
- Devices able to access Wix **wix.com**
- Reconstruction of Sir Tim Berners-Lee's first site at **http://info.cern.ch**
- 'What is the world wide web?' guide **bit.ly/pricomp055**
- 'How does the internet work?' guide **bit.ly/pricomp056**
- Access to a number of websites to compare, e.g. **bbc.co.uk/newsround**, **laughingsquid.com**, **classicfm.com**

Getting started
Inform your class that they are going to begin to learn how to design websites. Display a familiar site on the whiteboard, for example, the school website or a search engine. Press Ctrl and U, which on most browsers should bring up the source code for the site for the children to browse. Explain that behind every website there is code, but that there are many different ways to produce a website. Firstly, show the children an example of a modern website. Ask them to imagine what the first website looked like and what it was about. Show them the reconstruction of Sir Tim Berners-Lee's first website at **http://info.cern.ch**. Discuss with the class whether it met their expectations and ask them to compare how websites have evolved since that time. Browse the BBC guide, 'What is the world wide web?' at **bit.ly/pricomp055** and **bit.ly/pricomp056** for more information. Encourage your pupils to gaze into the future and think about how the Web might evolve.

Class activities: Sites for sore eyes
Ask the pupils to look at a selection of websites, such as **bbc.co.uk/newsround**, **laughingsquid.com**, **classicfm.com** and many more of your own examples.

Discuss as a class the features that most of the websites share, and features that are particular to how the individual website is used. For example, here are some common similarities:
- Logo – often in the top left corner
- Navigation menus – often near the top of the website
- Adverts – often animated
- Search box
- Sidebar – often on the right of the page
- Similar articles links – often under the main article or in the sidebar.

Give the pupils the brief that the school has been given a contract to design the website, branding, and source the products for a new toy company. The pupils will be working in pairs and will start by naming the company and designing a logo. They can design this digitally, or they can draw it and use a scanner to make a digital version. For the products, they can search Creative Commons free images or take photos of toys they have at home. Once all the material for the website has been gathered, including a draft of the text and a plan of the design, they can begin its construction.

Give the class a brief tour of Google Sites. Many of the simple functions are similar to Google Docs, such as adding and formatting images and text. In addition, users can select a layout to help structure the page by clicking on the 'layout' menu. Ask each pair to open Google Sites themselves and click on *Create site*. They will be prompted to name their site and to choose a theme. These can be changed later, but it is much easier to get it right now if possible. They will then begin to edit the home page by pressing the 'pen' *Edit* button. From their previous lessons on collaborative projects they will be familiar with most of the functions, as it is very similar to using documents in Google Drive. Encourage the pupils to explore the *Layout* menu, remembering the research they conducted before (see Getting started, p78) about how most websites look. Prompt the class to regularly save their websites so that they are not lost. Encourage your pupils to look at the various *Gadgets* that can be added to the page, and to explore whether any of these would make the website look more authentic. They can also use gadgets to embed videos and other media. Once the home page has been completed, instruct the class to make additional product pages to link to within the site.

Class activities: Designing for designers
Explain to the pupils that their last website was such a hit that you have decided that the class will start their own media company, designing websites. The next task is to design a website to advertise their services. Ask the pupils to work in pairs and research ideas for their new website. This time they will be using the website-designing tool at **wix.com**. Take the pupils on a tour of the website designer. As with the previous site, users are prompted to create a site name and to select a theme. The theme is particularly important, as a media company needs something that looks professional, so the class shouldn't be too quick to make a decision. Also, ensure that the pupils think about how the website looks and works on a mobile phone too. In their pairs, ask the pupils to adapt the template with their own company and product information, and add the contact details for the school. The pupils can add their own images to their site, but ensure that they follow savvy web user principles and don't share personal information. Once the homepage is complete, the pupils can choose to add and edit additional pages if they have the time, or they can leave them as they are.

Plenary
Create a simple and not well-designed class website on Google Sites, duplicate it, and ask the pupils to redesign and improve it. Ask your head teacher to judge the best version. Once a winner has been chosen, assign two pupils each week to maintain the site and keep it updated to run alongside the class blog.

Stage 3 Information and design

In the hectic digital age, information can be lost in the cacophony of competing voices, so media organisations are becoming more savvy with how information is presented online. One prominent technique is the rise of the infographic. This is a visually-pleasing poster showing information in bite-sized pieces. See some examples at **bit.ly/pricomp057**.

You will need
- A selection of infographics **bit.ly/pricomp057**
- Devices able to access **canva.com** and **clker.com**
- Devices able to access Google Drive **drive.google.com**
- Devices able to access **piktochart.com** or **easel.ly**

Getting started
Put up a sign on the classroom wall a few days before the lesson, which says something like, 'No running!', 'Remember! Have you put your name on your work?' or something else that drives you crazy about your class. Do this unannounced and see if (a) the pupils notice, and (b) it changes their behaviour.

When the lesson begins, ask the pupils about the sign and whether they think it made any difference to their behaviour. Discuss why or why not.

Class activities: Looking for a sign
Tell your class that you need their help to design a better sign to convey the same message, and that this time it will include reasons for following your 'suggestion'. Ask the pupils to offer ideas for why doing as the sign asks is a good idea. Note their ideas on the whiteboard and prompt for any ideas that you feel they have missed.

Ask them to quickly draft a simple design for the new sign on paper. Once complete, discuss some of the designs as a whole class, highlighting any images or lack thereof. Talk about why including graphics can improve engagement with a poster. Show the pupils a collection of infographics from either **bit.ly/pricomp057** or others you have found. Ask the pupils to choose two reasons to back up the classroom 'suggestion' and to design a poster using **canva.com**. Briefly show the pupils the main features of the website and explain that (on a teacher's salary) only the free items can be used. You can drag images from the categories section on the left of the page onto the canvas. Images can also be uploaded by the user, and text can be added. Encourage pupils to source further images via **clker.com** and show them how to upload them from their device. Give the pupils the login details, and allow them to design their poster, suggesting tweaks where necessary.

Class activities: Collaborative graphics
Ask the pupils to research facts about a topic they are learning about in the wider curriculum – a maths or science topic, or SPaG (Spelling, punctuation and grammar) rules, common mistakes and advice are all good areas to focus on. Divide the class into groups of six and instruct them to share computers in pairs. Open Google Drive and tell one pairing to open a new slide presentation and share it with the others. Infographics are usually long portrait posters and the children will need to change the page dimensions to emulate this. They can do this in page setup (*File > Page setup*). They should choose *Custom* size, and then change the second number to something much bigger. You will probably also need to adjust the *zoom* settings under the *View* menu. Next, ask the three sub-groups to begin work on

their educational graphic. Suggest that the pupils mainly work on different sections to avoid confusion, but have input if needed to improve and correct the other sections.

Class activities: Going green

A large environmental charity has commissioned the class to help them with their next promotional poster. See a template letter at **bit.ly/pricomp058** to download and personalise. The pupils will need to begin researching and thinking about the content before they start work on the graphic itself, making a note of any sources they plan to use.

Ask the pupils to go to **piktochart.com** or **easel.ly** and sign in. Briefly show them how the website works – it is very similar to Canva, with images and text being added to the canvas by dragging them in to place. Further onscreen help is available if needed.

Their infographics should include:
- A brand new logo for The Green Alliance
- Short case-study paragraphs
- Reasons to care for the environment
- Easy things that everyone can do to help the environment
- Links to any sources.

Plenary

Finally, ask the pupils to choose their preferred tool and to design an infographic about the school, including information about the history, ethos, current staff and yearly events and traditions. The graphics should be approximately A4 in dimension as one design will be chosen to feature in the next update of the school prospectus.

Useful links

bit.ly/pricomp059 Guide to designing Infographics.

Progression

The pupils have pushed further into the online space and have developed websites to create a permanent presence on the Web. They have used a range of collaborative tools to work with others and they have experienced real-time collaboration, as well as working on projects by taking turns, building on the expertise and skillset of their team.

Cross-curricular links

Collaboration opportunities can be seen across the primary curriculum, and collaborative writing is a wonderful activity to use in English, but it can also be used to refine explanations in science and the humanities. Creating forms in Google Drive has obvious links to maths, where data collection and analysis is a useful skill, but creating quizzes to reinforce their own collective learning is also very valuable. The same is true of collaborative presentations – these have unbound possibilities. Summarising information into easily digestible segments is an important learning skill, and infographic design techniques, whether online or hand-drawn sketch note form, help pupils consolidate their understanding and create reference materials that they can look back on later.

Year 4 e-Savvy

Focus: Spam and shopping

What do I need to know?

The advertising we meet online is unlike anything you find in the offline world. The promotions are tailored to your browsing habits and your interests, gathered from the trails left as you browse the Web. There are measures that can be taken to reduce the breadcrumbs we leave for corporations to feed on, such as using tools like *Epic Browser*, but most people don't bother. Many of the world's biggest tech companies exist to mine personal information about you in order to tailor services and products to your needs. Whether you believe this is the best form of bespoke customisation or a sinister plot to mess with your psychology to sell you things, being armed with knowledge about how this is achieved is vital.

The National Curriculum states that pupils in KS2 should:

- *Use technology safely, respectfully and responsibly; recognise acceptable/unacceptable behaviour; identify a range of ways to report concerns about content and contact.*
- *Use search technologies effectively, appreciate how results are selected and ranked, and be discerning in evaluating digital content.*

This section addresses using technology safely by understanding something of the commercial nature of the Web, and looks at protective measures to reduce the risks from spam.

> ### Interesting fact
>
> Around 50 percent of emails today are spam. This figure is down from just a few years ago when it was more than two thirds of emails. (BBC Technology, 2015)

Key words

Spam: Any unsolicited email, usually from commercial entities or scammers sending malicious code to infect your computer.

Stage 1 Spam, spam and spam

Email is safer than it used to be. Spam is still an everyday occurrence but it is becoming slightly less common, according to official figures (BBC Technology, 2015). A combination of better interception technology and the public becoming more savvy about avoiding it, after growing up with it over the past few decades, means that levels are slowly dropping. Despite the fact that people laugh about some spam, it is easy to forget one thing: it obviously works, otherwise the spammers wouldn't do it! Teach your pupils simple techniques to avoid falling for email scams and exercise their healthy scepticism.

You will need
- A school email system and an outside email account
- A group of currently gullible pupils
- Access to **bitly.com**
- Access to **milliondollarhomepage.com** (but don't click on anything!)

Getting started
A week or so before the lesson, create a non-school email account that uses a random string of letters and numbers as the username. Send out a typical spam email template message to your whole class, looking something like:

> Subject: Play free games forever online NOW

> Quick! Click the link at _____ to download free games.

> Offer ends today!

Sign in to **bitly.com** to create a disguised, short, random letter-and-number link to your school website or your class blog and add it to the blank space above. From the Bitly dashboard you will then be able to see how many of your pupils click on the link. Once the mock malicious email has been sent, send a real email from your own email address with a task or news that requires the pupils to check their email accounts – they will therefore be more likely to discover your phony spam email and respond.

   A few weeks later, when you have the planned lesson, check the number of clicks on the spam email link just before the lesson. Explain what you did with the spam email to the pupils and show them the graph of the number of clicks. Display a copy of the email on the whiteboard and, without naming names, discuss why this email is alluring.

Class activities: Fooling Year 6
Discuss what spammers hope to achieve when they send out emails:
- To sell you products and services – many legitimate companies mine or buy lists of email addresses and add them illegally to their mailing lists
- To try to trick you into replying to get personal information from you
- To install malicious software on your computer to take information, spy on you or make your computer send out more spam.

Brainstorm the pupils' ideas for combatting spam and make a note of them on the whiteboard. Make sure the following techniques are among them:
- If you don't recognise the sender, don't open it
- If the email has a generic subject title, don't open it

- If the email text is general and not specific to you, press the spam filter button to delete it and protect others
- If the email seems to be a newsletter that you have not signed up for, press the spam button – do not attempt to unsubscribe as the link may install software on your computer
- If the email is offering you something too good to be true…it's not
- Do not download attachments or click on links unless you completely trust the source
- Spam is often sent via a comprised email account, which can include your family, friends and colleagues – if an email from them looks suspicious, don't open it, don't click on any links, and don't download attachments; contact them using another communication method to check whether they sent it
- Don't reply to spam
- If you are concerned, alert an adult.

Without telling your pupils, assign each of them an older pupil (in Year 6) to spam via the school email system. Ensure that their teacher is aware of this activity, and hopefully the Year 6 children will be prepared, having completed the same activity at the same age. Ask your pupils to email their text to your non-school spamming account for you to check and send out with another traceable Bitly link. After a week, check the numbers and see if there have been any clicks.

Class activities: Explore the market

As I'm sure you've noticed, once you begin to browse for products in online stores you will begin to see similar items in adverts for the next few days. Take your pupils on a tour of online advertising: look at the promoted links at the top of the results of your search engine of choice; look at the non-intrusive promotions at **theguardian.com/education**; examine promoted tweets and hashtags on Twitter; view the over-video banners and pre-watch adverts on YouTube; and finally view the site at **milliondollarhomepage. com**, which revels in being just one big advertisement – but don't click on any of them! Of course, advertising is not just on the Web. Ask the pupils where else they see digital advertisements. For example, many free apps are supported by adverts.

Ask the pupils to design their idea of the perfect static online advertisement which will be irresistible not to click on. They can use tools such as **canva.com** or *Draw it!*. Place the advertisements in a public place somewhere in the school and add a piece of paper for pupils and staff to add their name under each example if they're interested in 'buying' or signing up to the product, in order to measure the success of the advertisements.

Class activities: School expansion

Tell the pupils that the school is considering expanding its numbers and they have been put in charge of the media campaign. Firstly, ask the pupils to interview the school business manager and some governors so they get a sense of what image the school, their 'client', wishes to portray. If you have anyone in the school community you can invite in or anyone who can Skype with your class, this would also be beneficial. Ask the pupils to design a simple digital advertisement to post to the school website to attract more pupils to the school.

Plenary

Reach out to local businesses and offer to design adverts for them, which could also appear in the school's newsletter as an added incentive for them to get involved. Ask the pupils to reflect on how their web-based behaviour has changed based on the work they have done about advertisements, and to blog their thoughts.

Stage 2 Online shopping

The days when you kept your money in a sock under your bed are fast becoming a distant memory. Now your money is in Google's sock and under Apple's bed. Using contactless payment cards is gaining popularity, and paying via mobile wallets is becoming more and more common. The world of commerce has been changing quickly since the Web was born, and trillions of pounds of assets are bought, sold, traded and speculated on each day. In this stage, your class will begin learning about finance with no money at all!

You will need
- A range of online stores
- Devices able to access **UKEd.Directory**
- Devices able to access Google Drive **drive.google.com**

Getting started
Visit a range of online stores and look at how they work. Ask the pupils to remain signed out as they browse, search and add items to the basket. Look at the product descriptions, product suggestions and purchasing options.

Discuss the pros and cons of shopping online compared to shopping on the high street, including ease of browsing, when you receive your items, choice, and security.

Class activities: Go shopping
There are few safe environments for children to practise online shopping; however, UKEdChat's teaching resource directory is built on an online store template, but has open-access teaching resources to download. Ask the pupils to visit **uked.directory** and to sign in using the shared details of an account you have set up before the lesson. Ask the pupils to browse the free items, add some to their basket and then follow the instructions to download the resources. Ask the pupils to repeat this a few times to get the idea. Ask all pupils to find the *School Stocks* resource on the directory, which is a Google Drive-based resource. Ask them to make a copy of the resource in their own drive (*File > Make a copy*) and to share it with you ready for the next activity.

Class activities: Playing the market
Your pupils should have added the School Stocks resource to their Google Drive. This is a virtual stock exchange for your pupils to practise managing pretend stock. Each day the stock price for each company will change, and company news and expert opinion will be published periodically. Ask the pupils to make their investments each school day.

At the end of the week or month count up remaining stock and declare a winner.

Plenary
Talk about potential security concerns surrounding shopping online, e.g. companies can be hacked and smaller unknown retailers need to gain your trust just like a stranger becoming a friend. Ask your pupils to gaze into the future and think about what online shopping will be like when they are older. Also, discuss the rise of new digital currencies, like BitCoin (see BBC video clip and information at **bit.ly/pricomp060**).

Progression

Over the two stages the pupils have learnt to be savvy web users, despite being continuously bombarded with the pressure to click and buy. They have also learnt valuable strategies to keep safe when spam and malicious emails hit their inbox.

Cross-curricular links

The first stage has many connections to art and design, with many creative decisions and designs needed to complete the projects. The second stage has many links to maths, and personal and social development.

Year 4 Coding

Focus: Python and developing games

What do I need to know?

Numbers and code go hand in hand. You and your pupils will no doubt have noticed the increasing amount of maths in the code they have been developing, but now it is time to bring numbers to the fore and make them a part of the project itself, with variables, points and scoring. But before that, we will explore a coding game built on new coding language.

The National Curriculum states that pupils in KS2 should:

- *Design, write and debug programs that accomplish specific goals, including controlling or simulating physical systems; solve problems by decomposing them into smaller parts.*
- *Use sequence, selection and repetition in programs; work with variables and various forms of input and output.*
- *Use logical reasoning to explain how some simple algorithms work and to detect and correct errors in algorithms and programs.*

This section will cover all of these strands, with a particular focus on variables, inputs and outputs.

> ### Interesting fact
>
> The creator of the programming language 'Python', Guido Van Rossum, named it after the popular 1970s cult comedy sketch show, *Monty Python's Flying Circus*[4]. 'Python' often uses famous Monty Python references in its code, such as 'spam' and 'eggs'![5]

Key words

Variables: An element of code that can change its value to give different input to other pieces of code.

---

4 "General Python FAQ". *Python v2.7.3 documentation.* Docs.python.org. Retrieved 11 March 2016.
5 "Whetting Your Appetite". *The Python Tutorial.* Python Software Foundation. Retrieved 11 March 2016.

Stage 1 Taming the python

We have met many different coding languages so far. It is important that the children have a wide range of experience with all of these coding languages at this stage so to keep their options open for secondary school and beyond. Furthermore, programming languages are not used in isolation and not all are equally suited for any given task. In this stage we will meet Python, one of the easiest coding languages to learn.

You will need
• Devices that can access **codecombat.com**

Getting started
Begin with a game of *Code this*, which is a variation on the game *Simon says*. In this game, instead of saying 'Simon says...' you give coded commands for the pupils to follow. The instructions either begin with, 'Code self...' (for actions) or 'Code this...' (for speech). Use the following coded commands, which are based on the Python programming language that you are going to be covering in this stage, and add to them with your own variations. The actual code is also shown for your reference. If you don't say the word 'Code' at the start of your command, the pupils should not follow the instructions! If they do, they are out.

Instruction	Command	Python code
Move right	Code self move right	self.moveRight()
Move left	Code self move left	self.moveLeft()
Say 'hello'	Code this say 'Hello'	this.say("Hello")

Figure 4A: 'Code this' instructions

Class activity: Battle with python
Before the lesson, sign your class up to their own *Code Combat* accounts via **codecombat. com**. The levels are extensive and if your pupils continue through all the levels they will have an excellent grounding in Python coding. As with most code, it is important to use the correct syntax and capitalisation.

To survive and prosper over the first ten levels of *Code Combat,* your pupils just need to know the basic movements:

    self.moveUp()
    self.moveDown()
    self.moveLeft()
    self.moveRight()

They also need to know two actions:

    self.attack("Name")
    self.say("Something")

They will also need to know how to repeat an algorithm using a loop command:

    while True:

These and many more commands are prompted for when they are needed and there are help tutorials on screen and in the help area if you or your pupils get stuck. Also, one word of advice: encourage your pupils to only make equipment power-ups when absolutely necessary, as they may not have the virtual cash to buy needed items. So, pick up your sword and battle with code!

Plenary
Once the children have battled to around level ten, ask them to play the game *Code this* again (see Getting started, p88). This time, ask one of the pupils to call out the commands. Their understanding will certainly have improved.

Useful links

checkio.org Checkio Python coding game.
pygame.org PY game.

Stage 2 Varied activities

One of the core principles of gaming is trying to achieve a high score. Changing numbers and other qualities are called 'variables' and they can feed inputs into other parts of the code to bring about changes to the game or product.

You will need
- Devices able to access Scratch **scratch.mit.edu**
- BBC guide and video, 'How do computer programs use variables?' **bit.ly/pricomp061**
- Behaviour chart example **bit.ly/pricomp062**
- Catch simulator **bit.ly/pricomp063**
- Timer example **bit.ly/pricomp064**

Getting started
In an open space, turn your pupils into robots that obey your every command (sorry, only temporarily!). Ask them to move around the space in slow motion and inform them that this is 'speed 1'. Ask them to walk at normal pace as 'speed 5' and a jog will be 'speed 10'. Explore making them accelerate from speed 0 to various speeds and decelerate. Repeat the activity for voice volume control, height of walking control (e.g. from army crawl to tall walking), width of walking control (from walking thin to spreading arms out to make themselves walk wide), and a combination of all of them.

Class activities: Points mean programs
Open a new Scratch project on the whiteboard computer. The following activities will introduce the blocks in the orange *Data* and green *Operators* categories.
- Add a *when ____ key pressed* trigger from the *Events* feature and then go to *Data* and *Make a Variable*.
- Call the variable *score*.
- You will also have a choice of whether to make the variable available to just the currently selected sprite or whether you want all sprites to interact with this variable. If you give every variable a unique name you can keep your options open and make it available for all sprites.
- Drag the *change score by 1* block under your trigger and press your chosen key. The score will increase each time you press the key.
- Ask the pupils to copy this sequence, then ask them to make a keyboard key reset the score back to zero – using *set score to 0* is a good block to use for this.
- Next, ask the pupils to add the flag trigger to a sprite followed by the *Forever* loop from the *Control* feature, and inside that place a forward motion block followed by a short *wait* and then *if on edge, bounce* block
- Place the *score* oval block into the motion's number.
- Finally, drag a *change score by 1* block into the algorithm (see Figure 4B on the following page). What you should find is that your sprite moves across the screen in bigger and bigger jumps, giving the impression of getting faster. Use the keyboard code to reset the score variable.

Figure 4B: Bounce variable

Class activities: Gravity

Simulating gravity is tricky in games, but you can make a simple version if you try the following code. (Actually, the code is really rapid acceleration downwards rather than gravity.)

• Remove everything inside the *forever* loop, and then drag in the code shown in Figure 4C below. Note that in the green operator the code is to multiply the score number by five – in coding a * replaces the usual multiplication sign.

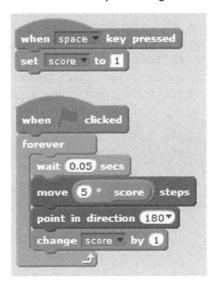

Figure 4C: Fake gravity

• Pick up the sprite and drag it to the top of the screen, ensure the score variable has been reset, and then run the code. The sprite should drop to the bottom.
• Ask the pupils to explore what changing each of the variables does by remixing the code.

Class activities: Time

Ask the pupils to create a stopwatch and countdown using variables. They may wish to graphically represent the passage of time, use numbers from the library or attempt to draw a clock face. See the example at **bit.ly/pricomp064**. They will need to include a *repeat* loop and *wait* intervals to ensure the clock ticks. See the example in Figure 4D below.

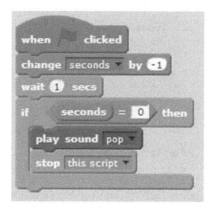

Figure 4D: Timer

Once they have designed a countdown clock, ask the pupils to include a mechanism to alert the user that the clock has run out. They can build alert code or even animate a cuckoo to pop out of their timer.

Class activities: Random motion

Ask the pupils to explore the *random* operator. Ask them to input a range and add in various motion blocks with a trigger. Encourage them to add random numbers to *move* and *turn* blocks. Ask them to try the coordinate block too. Show them the sequence below (Figure 4E) to give random movement anywhere on the stage.

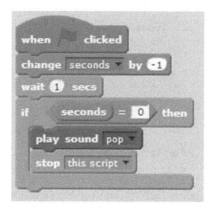

Figure 4E: Random motion

The sprite will now dart across the stage to random positions very quickly.

Suggest the pupils make a mini game of 'Catch the sprite'. Start a new sequence with a *when this sprite clicked* trigger and a *change score by 1* variable. Now every time they are able to click on the sprite, the score will increase. Ask the pupils to save their project so they can refer back to the code for the next project.

Class activities: Charting success

Ask the pupils to design a reward/behaviour chart for themselves and three of their classmates. Divide the class into groups of four in register order for this activity, although you can adjust the number to fit with the number of children in your class. Suggest that each pupil is represented by a different sprite. For your reference, see **bit.ly/pricomp062**, but do not show this to the children until they have started down their own design path. Instead of simply adding numbers as in the example, they may wish to represent the scores graphically, e.g. by moving the sprites across the screen in a race. Prompt the pupils to consider more than one behaviour as a variable. Once the children near the end of their projects, encourage them to swap ideas and view other groups' projects so that they might refine their ideas.

Class activities: Drawing

The final category we are exploring in this section is the pen blocks – these allow you to add a line traced out from your sprite. Instruct the pupils to use *pen down* to start drawing and *pen up* to stop drawing on the stage.

Ask the pupils to create two sprites and design a project where they play a game of catch, with a third sprite being the ball, and leaving pen lines in between them. Suggest the pupils add some randomness and make sure to *pen up* if the ball goes outside a given coordinate line behind the catcher, using the *if…then* control block. Use the *glide to coordinates* block to return the ball to the thrower. See an example at **bit.ly/pricomp063**.

Try a similar simulation with flying sprites. See if the pupils can write an algorithm that can write their name.

Plenary

Bring together all the skills from the above activities by asking pupils to make a sprite bounce across the screen with a pen trail using random numbers so the bounces change slightly each time. Change this into a stone-skimming mini game.

Why make games?

Games are fun, and creating your own is even more so. Coding is a pursuit that requires problem-solving skills, forward-thinking and planning, persistence and lots of creativity. It is also wonderfully cross-curricular: any subject or topic area can be the material for a game, to consolidate the learning of both the coder and the players.

The British gaming sector is a multi-billion pound industry for which the country has a proud tradition, and it is a sector that is growing fast. According to an article in *The Telegraph* in 2009, video games were already then outselling films (Wallop, 2009). The economy is desperately short of good programmers and as a result wages are high, job satisfaction is high and the opportunities are truly global – and unlikely to change by the time your pupils grow up.

Stage 3 Game on

Games are an amazingly motivating way to get children coding, as I'm sure you have seen. In this stage we are putting together all the skills the pupils have learnt so far to create some fun games.

You will need
- Devices that can access Scratch **scratch.mit.edu**
- BBC guide and videos, 'What makes a good computer game?' **bit.ly/pricomp065**
- Beginnings of a battle game **bit.ly/pricomp066**
- Example of a driving game **bit.ly/pricomp067**
- Another racing game **bit.ly/pricomp068**
- Example of a platform game **bit.ly/pricomp069**
- Example of scrolling effect **bit.ly/pricomp070**
- Example of walking between scenes **bit.ly/pricomp071**

Getting started
The only block category the pupils haven't explored in detail yet in Scratch is sensing, which we will cover in Year 5 (p114). Ask the pupils to browse Scratch and to pick out a few games that they not only really like but also, after looking inside the code, think they can use to make a similar game. Look at the code yourself and shortlist this down to three types of games:
- Battle games
- Racing games
- Platform games.

Tell the class that you don't want them to remix existing games made by the community, but they can use the *Backpack* code storage area to gather snippets of code that they think might be useful. Show the BBC guide and videos, 'What makes a good computer game?' at **bit.ly/pricomp065** to the class, reminding them about the importance of decomposition.

Class activities: Let battle begin
Ask all of the pupils to add a character sprite and something to throw onto the stage. They should code the arrow keys as triggers to change the direction of the sprite character and the direction of the projectile. Suggest they use costumes and wait to animate the throwing object. Ensure that the object disappears after a few seconds or the screen will be full of them. They can also add an *if on edge, bounce* block to change the game play, if required.

Once the pupils have had some time attempting this by themselves, allow them to see the example at **bit.ly/pricomp066**. Ask the pupils to develop this into a two-player battle game using variables to keep score. Suggest that they add obstacles and 'capture the flag' goals to add extra game play.

Class activities: On the level
One tricky aspect of gaming to get right with Scratch is rolling backgrounds. Unless it is vital to the game, I would suggest your pupils use a static backdrop, as the process of making them move requires many backdrops whooshing past in sequence, using variables to coordinate them. Having said that, it is important for the pupils to see what is possible. An example of a rolling background can be seen at **bit.ly/pricomp070**. Ask the pupils

to copy a remix of the project into their account in order to experiment and tweak the code. Discuss the difficulties and possible alternatives. The pupils might consider walking between scenes like the classic problem-solving adventure game, *Another World* (see video at **bit.ly/pricomp072**) and like the simple example at **bit.ly/pricomp070** to give the illusion of extra space.

Class activities: Driving

Driving games have been a staple since the first home computers, and they can be very easy to make. In this first example at **bit.ly/pricomp067**, the code is simply tilting the road and moving it around in a slightly random fashion. The game is to just keep the car on the road using the arrow keys. Ask your class to develop this idea by adding a scoring system using variables, other motorists to avoid, additional game play, and extra scenery.

Another idea for making a driving game is to design a racing game – looking down from above the cars makes coding easier. Use an accelerator variable to control the speed of the cars, like in the example at **bit.ly/pricomp068**, and ask the pupils to add in triggers to control the steering. In the example above there is just a single map screen, but ask the pupils to use multiple static scenes where the car drives between backdrops like the previous dungeon example. You can suggest that the pupils try the technique to make a cityscape driving area and make an age-appropriate version of the game *Grand Theft Auto*. Add a variable to count the number of laps. They can even add special effects like going over a ramp and simulating going into the air by growing the sprite and shrinking it again as it touches the ground.

Plenary

The pupils are now creating real games with real rules, scores, levels and game play. To bring all this together, the pupils are going to do some market research into the types of games children in KS1 like to play and then make a bespoke game for that age group. They will then embed the HTML code into a Google site, create a traceable Bitly link and create an advert to email to Years 1 and 2 to invite them to play, using many of the skills and platforms they have learnt about during their Year 4 computing lessons.

Progression

The pupils have learnt basic Python, a commonly-used programming language. They have learnt how output and input variables can be used to make games responsive and interactive, and how to manipulate variables and other code using maths with operators. The pupils have also gained further knowledge of decomposition of tasks into bite-sized pieces for the computer to digest, and they have practised their debugging skills to develop and build on existing projects and code.

Cross-curricular links

It hasn't been the main focus in the activities above; however, games can be educational and they can focus on any area of the primary curriculum. The aspects of coding covered have strong links with maths of all kinds, particular number theory, with the operator blocks being pure maths. There have also been links to product design – which links to design and technology, and art.

Year 5 Using and understanding computing

Focus: Mapping and 3D design

What do I need to know?

Technology now allows us to scale mountains and explore cities around the world from the relative comfort of the classroom. Mapping applications give us the opportunity to peer down at any point on the planet, and we can virtually walk down streets in distant parts of the world. The educational value of seeing the neighbourhoods, backstreets and landscape vistas of distant places simply cannot be overstated. In my opinion, the development in mapping is one of the greatest gifts technology has given to educators, and it has given us unprecedented power to dispel stereotypes and understand other cultures by standing in distant streets and mingling in far-off public places.

In the first stage of this section, your pupils will begin a virtual exploration of the world using digital mapping tools. In the final stages, your class will develop skills to fill the world with both real and virtual artefacts. They will explore 3D printing design, designing buildings and other objects using SketchUp, and building almost anything in Minecraft.

The National Curriculum states that pupils in KS2 should:

- *Understand computer networks including the internet; how they can provide multiple services, such as the world wide web; and the opportunities they offer for communication and collaboration.*
- *Select, use and combine a variety of software (including internet services) on a range of digital devices to design and create a range of programs, systems and content that accomplish given goals, including collecting, analysing, evaluating and presenting data and information.*

This section will address aspects of both strands, but particularly the second strand as the children use software to design 3D objects and environments, and use and analyse data in mapping platforms.

Interesting fact

The clocks on board the Global Positioning System (GPS) satellites need to be calibrated to account for Einstein's theory of general relativity, which states that for bodies with greater relative motion, time moves more slowly. The chronometers are so finely tuned that this small effect would mean that the position readings would drift by several metres per day if corrections were not made.[6]

---

6 Source: www.astronomy.ohio-state.edu/~pogge/Ast162/Unit5/gps.html

Key words

3D printing: A generic term used for many different processes in which material is built up in three dimensions over time (referred to as additive manufacturing or rapid prototyping technologies), in order to make physical objects from computer designs.
CAD: Computer-aided design, often used when designing digital objects to 3D print.

Stage 1 Mapping

Maps are an amazing resource to display data and make locations, information and interactions more meaningful. Cartography has held a special place in our culture since ancient times, yet despite the long history and importance to trade, politics and travel, accurate mapping is a fairly recent phenomenon. Satellites have made the map-making process so much easier, but because the image resolution of commercial satellites is still limited, most of the aerial map images you use on your computer and smartphone are likely to be taken by aircraft. Even that level of precision isn't enough though, and now humans in cars, and more recently drones (see more in Year 6, p123), now map individual streets and some of the more wild places all around the world.

You will need
- A local paper A–Z road atlas or map and/or Ordnance Survey map
- Access to Old Maps Online **oldmapsonline.org**
- Access to GeoGuessr **geoguessr.com**
- Devices able to access Google Maps **maps.google.com**
- Geocaching equipment, e.g. small plastic waterproof boxes, paper and permanent markers
- A globe and some pipe cleaners
- Access to Knit **trebleapps.co/knit**
- Access to What 3 Words **map.what3words.com**
- Access to Earth data at **earth.nullschool.net**

Getting started
Begin by looking at a paper A–Z map of your local area. Encourage the pupils (although not much encouragement will be needed) to find their street and other local features that they know. Point out common features that are found on most maps, such as the grid reference, a key, the scale, etc.

Next, show a historical map of the local area by using the map search engine at **oldmapsonline.org** – display it on the whiteboard for the pupils to marvel at. You may wish the pupils to take a closer look, either on their own device or a printed version. Check the individual site's terms about printing the image first. As before, ask the pupils to find their street, or the absence of it on the map, and other details. You may also wish to look at **historypin.org** and **britainfromabove.org.uk** for additional material.

Class activities: My maps

Ask the pupils to visit Google Maps at **maps.google.com**. Allow them plenty of time to explore and discover things about their local area and beyond. Ask them to switch between *Map* and *Earth view*. Also tell them to open the tab on the left of the screen and to explore the *Earth*, *Traffic* and *Terrain* options.

Next, tell the pupils to drag the yellow stick figure onto the map from the bottom right corner of the screen. The map will change into *Street View* mode and the children will be able to wander around the streets of many towns and cities around the world. Take this opportunity to visit some of the world's unique historic and cultural sites – you can also explore the *Photo Spheres* and *See Inside* imagery areas too.

Be ready to hear your pupils gasp as you ask them to use the tilt map setting under the compass in *Earth view* – the map becomes 3D, looking very similar to the tilt shift photos we explored in Year 1 (p8). Not every location has been rendered in 3D, so if your town is looking a little flat, visit London or New York's Manhattan to see the buildings pop out at you.

Ask the pupils to explore creating their own map.

- Ensure the pupils are signed in to their Google accounts and ask them to look in the menu tab on the left side of the page, and find and click on *My Maps*.
- Press *Create Map* at the bottom of that window, which should open a new browser tab.
- Next you have two choices: either ask the pupils to search for places relevant to a topic you are doing in the wider curriculum, or you can ask them to plot places they have been to and/or like and insert them into their own collection of places. While the map should be private, ask them not to make their house one of these for their own e-safety.
- They can either find the places manually by zooming in to the location, or they can use the search bar. Remember, many places around the world share names, so some additional search terms, such as the county and 'UK', may be useful.
- Ask the pupils to add up to five markers – these look like an upside down teardrop – to their maps in their chosen locations. Note that for each marker you should be able to see the GPS coordinates, which we will come to later.
- Next, instruct them to click the ruler tool, near the search bar at the top of the page. They will measure the distance between the points in what they believe is the shortest distance and back to the first point again, making a note of each measurement as they go.

Class activities: Geocaching and orienteering

Geocaching is essentially a high-tech version of hide and seek. The idea is not to hide yourself, but to hide a cache item in a particular location and then publish the GPS coordinates for others to find. The cache can be anything from a badge or stickers to a message containing the location of further caches.

For your purposes, a piece of paper inside a small waterproof plastic box for finders to write their first names on will be sufficient. Writing a short message on the outside of the box in permanent marker, explaining what the box is doing there and to not move it, is helpful in case someone stumbles across it. Think carefully about where to place each box. You can ask members of the community to place a box in their front gardens, if they don't mind your pupils being amongst their petunias.

Once the box(es) are in place, send a letter home explaining the activity and ask that parents accompany their children to some of the geocache locations as homework. Include the coordinates in the letter and give any other relevant additional information, such as that the garden owners are expecting you to enter their garden. The pupils then use home or school devices to track down the items, either using live GPS or making a note of the approximate location from a computer and then setting out to look afterwards.

You can ask the pupils to complete the tracking in a particular order, add waypoints, and include non-GPS landmarks and other clues to bring in more orienteering skills. Discuss with your class about how GPS satellite signals allow triangulation of position to give one's location. A nice way to demonstrate this is with a classroom globe, some pipe cleaners and a few of your pupils as volunteers to hold the pipe cleaners from their satellite hands all pointing to the same location.

Knit **trebleapps.co/knit** is an iOS app that allows you to leave geo-based virtual messages for other users to find, which gives you the opportunity to geocache without a physical cache. (Also see the augmented reality section in Year 6, p129).

Class activities: Discovering the world

They've played hide and seek, but now the pupils can try the opposite and get dropped in the middle of nowhere and have to try to figure out where they are. No, this isn't some new harsh behaviour management technique or a test of the limits of their mindset mentality, this is **geoguessr.com** – an online mapping game. The website and app works by dropping the player in a Street View location somewhere in the world. The user scores points by guessing where in the world they are. The website does this randomly in five different places and the player must explore their surrounds, look for clues such as street and shop signs, and then make a guess on the map for where they think they are. You can also sign up to a GeoGuessr account to make your own challenges, where you can choose the locations for the pupils to guess. It's a wonderful way to explore the world and get a sense of what other countries look like once you are off the beaten track.

Of course, GPS coordinates are not the only way to find a location and there are many ingenious ways that people have divided up the globe. One fun website and app is **map. what3words.com**, which divides the whole world into 3m x 3m squares and assigns each square three random words. Ask your class to convert GPS coordinates into words, which you could use to make example SPaG sentences. Point out to pupils that much of the world's population doesn't have a postal address.

Class activities: It's raining data

Maps can be layered with data and your class will have noticed the place names, historical sites, restaurants and shops that can be seen on many online mapping applications that we have already examined. Yet some maps take adding information to a whole new level, and **earth.nullschool.net** is one such website. It shows an interactive 3D globe for your pupils to rotate, zoom in on and explore. The default screen is of the weather systems and air currents around the globe, and your pupils will instantly realise why we have the weather we do when they see the almost permanent strong weather systems heading our way across the North Atlantic. Ask your pupils to click on *Earth* text at the bottom left of the screen. This will present many more data options, including animated predictions of future weather patterns. Ask the pupils to use this data to put together some notes to make a weather forecast. Display the website on your whiteboard and ask the children to conduct the forecast in front, capturing it on video. A few days later, play the video back and see if the forecast was right.

Plenary
To bring all of their map work together, ask the pupils to design a virtual tour of the school by importing a map image into a Google slide presentation and creating hotspot links to other slides showing photos of that location of the school. Add linked arrows into the photos slides so users can navigate between the rooms as they can on Street View.

Useful links

openstreetmap.org Explore Street Mapping

Stage 2 3D design and manufacturing

3D printing is a catch-all term used for many different technologies and techniques. 'Additive manufacturing' and 'rapid prototyping' are two other terms that are used. These all involve designing a 3D object on a computer and building the object up, layer by layer, until it is complete. This is very different to traditional casting or sculpting techniques, as the layering process allows much greater precision and gives great flexibility over internal structures and spaces. You can even produce products with moving parts already assembled, such as gearing and hinge systems already in place. Furthermore, there are no joins, meaning that the structure is stronger for the amount of material used.

Having said this, additive manufacturing might be older then you think. The first pioneers of the technique began in the 1980s, printing using plastic, metals, wood from wood pulp and even foodstuffs.

3D printers are becoming an increasingly common sight in secondary schools in their art and DT departments, but they will be coming to primary schools too. After all, if the experts are right, in a few years, time advanced 3D printers will replace your stock cupboard as you will be able to make anything you need as easily as using the photocopier.

You will need
- Devices able to access AutoDesk **projectignite.autodesk.com** and Tinkercad **tinkercad.com**
- Devices able to run SketchUp **sketchup.com**

Getting started
Give the pupils a pot of play dough and ask them to build a range of simple objects, such as a person, a tree, a house, etc. Then, ask the children to design something much more intricate, such as the interior of the classroom. Suggest that they break up the play dough into tiny balls and add them in a row to build up the scene. Stop them fairly quickly and explain that this is essentially what a 3D printer does.

Class activities: Designing objects
AutoDesk has a superb suite of sites and apps to explore for 3D design. This kind of designing is often referred to as computer aided design (CAD). Firstly, ask your pupils to

experiment with the **tinkercad.com** platform and explore its capabilities. Ask them to design simple geometric shapes and to try to join them together. Next, tell your class to open the 'moon' project on Project Ignite (**bit.ly/pricomp073**) and to follow the on-screen instructions, which take them through making a large sphere and adding craters and colour. Suggest the pupils complete more of the projects on the site.

If your school doesn't have a 3D printer of its own, find out if a local secondary school does and get your class invited along to watch it in action – and hopefully to print a few of the CAD creations your class made.

Class activities: Sketching buildings and more

SketchUp, which was once part of Google, is a remarkable 3D design suite that was originally developed as an architecture tool to create buildings in Google maps. It is still used to design buildings, but you can now design anything. When the program is started for the first time, click on *templates* and choose *metres* to avoid the children working in imperial units.

Once a new SketchUp file is opened, your pupils will be given a blank canvas and a model person acting as a size reference. There will be a tutorial window on the right-hand side of the screen offering your pupils advice. Ensure that the children are aware of it.

Help the pupils become familiar with the software by guiding them through the following procedures.

- First of all, ask the pupils to draw a rectangle on the ground, using the *Rectangle* tool and clicking and dragging it across the virtual floor. This will create what looks like a rug on the floor.
- Instruct your pupils to locate the *Pull/Push* tool ('P' on the keyboard). They should move the mouse into the middle of the rug, click and then pull the floor upwards towards the top of the screen. They should now have a box and the beginnings of a house.
- Ask the pupils to make additional rectangles on the surface of the house and to push them in to create doors and windows. Use the *Pan* ('H' key) and *Orbit* ('O' key) commands to move around the object.
- Next to the *Rectangle* tool is a menu arrow. Click this to find more shapes. Ask the pupils to select *Circle* and to draw one on the virtual floor. Use the *Pull/Push* tools to create a cylinder for a lamp post.
- Find the *Paint Bucket* tool and ask the pupils to look in the folders and select choices, textures and materials to decorate their house.
- Ask the pupils to experiment with the *Move* and the *Rotate* tools on surfaces, on lines and on the corners of the building. They will notice that whatever is selected will be the thing that moves or rotates. They can use Ctrl and Z to undo any unfavourable changes this causes. For example, to make a pitched roof, instruct the pupils to draw a line down the middle of the currently flat roof from one side to the other. Use the black arrow *Select* tool to select the new line. Then use the *Move* tool to make the line higher. This should pitch in the middle of the roof, making equal angled lines.

Your pupils now have the basic skills to design a structure. Next, give them a specific task, drawn from work from the wider curriculum. Otherwise, ask them to make an accurate copy of the school building(s), including decorating it with the right materials. Once complete, ask the pupils to make a second copy of their design using *Save As* and then they can begin to redesign the school piece by piece to show how they think it can be improved.

Plenary

Using 3D designing suites to produce unique and bespoke products will become ubiquitous in the coming years, and the skills to design items will become ever more important in industry and for domestic uses. Ask your pupils to conduct research into products that members of Years 3 and 4 are interested in. Use the *Warehouse* area of SketchUp to find a suitable product as a starting point for designing, and then ask them to tweak it based on the needs of the intended Y3/4 owner. Repeatedly take the design back to the younger child to refine the design and then make more tweaks until it is finished.

Useful links

bit.ly/pricomp074 YouTube video about 3D printing.

Stage 3 Working in the sandbox

One of the first toys that we give our children is building blocks. The urge to build, design and create art is in us all. Minecraft is a wholly remarkable game. It is what game developers call a sandbox game, where there are few rules and open-ended goals, and it provides an area to create and explore. There are two main modes in Minecraft:

- Survival mode – where your resources are limited and you must fend off monsters while you search for items and build
- Creative mode – where your resources are unlimited and the aim is to build, design and collaborate.

Creative mode is the one that interests me for educational purposes, although teaching life and survival skills are also of value in Survival mode.

Think of Minecraft as an infinite virtual Lego™ set. A Minecraft world is effectively infinite and will keep on being generated as you move through it. A lot has been said about the addictive nature of Minecraft in the media, and it is…very! But you will need to make your own judgement about whether it is a bad thing if children become obsessed with collaborative creative design. After all, some Scandinavian countries now have Minecraft as a mandatory part of the curriculum for all pupils.

As teachers, we do find that there are certain areas of life for which some pupils will have a much better understanding than ourselves: street slang, pop music and work/life balance are just a few examples. Another will be Minecraft. In successive recent class cohorts, I have had pupils who play Minecraft habitually, stopping only for the occasional bite to eat. They use their expertise to help and guide others. However, despite the fact that they thoroughly know how to play the game, that doesn't mean that they have nothing to learn. For example, they may not have worked as a collaborative team before, having largely set their own goals up until now.

There are many different versions of Minecraft, including a version for smartphones, gaming consoles and even the Raspberry Pi, but the following lesson ideas will be focusing on the full PC version.

You will need
- One or more Minecraft accounts **minecraft.net**
- YouTube video, 'Minecraft timelapse – the land of Akane' **bit.ly/pricomp075**
- A local server or a Minecraft Realm
- Infinite time to build your infinite worlds

Getting started
Firstly, if you are in any doubt about the educational value of Minecraft, watch the YouTube video, 'Minecraft timelapse – the land of Akane' (**bit.ly/pricomp073**) with your class. Ask the pupils to share and discuss their own experiences of Minecraft and talk about the things they have built.

Before the pupils start working in Minecraft itself, you need to consider how you wish to set it up. There are three options:
1. Play the single-player game with each pupil in their own world (as usual)
2. Play the multi-player game on the school server
3. Play the multi-player game using a Minecraft Realm – this allows the pupils to enter the world from anywhere; it requires a subscription, but a trial period is available.

Part of the value of Minecraft is the collaborative element, so I would avoid the single-player option, unless you want to just demonstrate something or ask the pupils to explore the basics. In the first instance, hosting multi-player worlds on your local school server will be sufficient until you know Minecraft a little better.

Class activities: Finding the way
Ask the pupils to start Minecraft and to navigate to the particular world you want them to explore in *creative mode*. Ask them to explore the immediate area and to use the *break* function to smash blocks, cut down a few trees, etc. Ensure they know how to navigate, by using:
- WASD keys for movement
- The mouse for looking and changing direction
- The space bar for jumping.

Once the children have got the hang of the terrestrial movements, ask them to tap the space bar quickly twice. They should now be hovering. If they click the spacebar again they will go higher, and they can press shift to fly lower. Double tap the spacebar to return to the ground. Flying is fundamental to Minecraft as this allows you to build upwards more easily than building scaffolding blocks to reach high places.

> Warning: children have a habit of zooming off and getting lost as soon as they learn they can fly. Use the compass to navigate back to the 'spawning' location where they first appeared.

Class activities: Building skills
Draw the pupils' attention to the Hotbar – the nine item squares at the bottom of the screen. This contains the items you have quick access to. Ask the pupils to press the number keys on the keyboard to swap the selected item. The children can change the quick-access items by opening the inventory by pressing the E key. Press the number slot while hovering over the item you want. The items are divided into categories, including building blocks, decoration blocks, tools and many more.

Explain that Redstone items are like a power source in the game and have many uses, including lighting dark places. Ask the pupils to swap over some items and use the right mouse button to place blocks around them in the landscape.

Class activities: Destruction and construction

Before building a structure, encourage the pupils to create a cleared area, which doesn't slope too much. Next, ask the children to collaborate in teams to build a simple house. Encourage them to make it two storeys high. Inexperienced players often use just one material for building. Ask the pupils to decorate their house with appropriate colours and materials.

Tell the pupils that this building is a farmhouse, and that next they need to create a large area for some animals and to capture them by luring them with food. This is a great collaborative problem-solving task, as the animals don't always cooperate.

Ask the teams of pupils to begin to plan out a village with open spaces to walk through, but relatively close to make it a single settlement. As a whole class, brainstorm possible amenities that a village might have. If you wish to practise some village politics, then form a village council to set priorities and delegate tasks.

Naturally, a school is an important structure to include. Ask the pupils to design the best school in the world (other than your own of course), with all the latest technology and superb facilities.

Class activities: Grand designs

Engineering and planning are essential for good development. Using the right material and good structures for the task are key skills and good to practise in this virtual environment.

Ask the pupils to research some of the grandest houses and the most impressive world cultural sights. Ask them to build you a huge palace befitting your status as the benevolent overlord of this blocky domain. Ensure that the pupils work together to build you your own palace of Versailles, but nicer, with high-ceilinged halls and beautifully decorated interiors. Remind your class that you expect the green surroundings to be equally nice. They should question you on your preferences and refine the design based on your feedback as the future tenant.

While this is a nice little country home, what you and your townspeople want is a city. Ask the pupils to research the Manhattan skyline and to design a city with functioning buildings with internal levels, lifts that one can fly up and down, parks and transport links – including bridges over the water. Instruct the pupils to research what some of the tallest buildings in the world look like and to try to copy their designs into the city if possible. Ask the pupils to scout for a suitable location near a large body of water and then to begin building.

Suggest that the pupils develop the transport links further by building an underground tube network for the city. To do this, they will have to dig tunnels, design underground platforms, add tracks and make suitable access to the surface. Ask the pupils to build boats and even giant cruise ships in the water. Challenge the children to build objects in the sky, such as airplanes and even an international space station. Blocks can only be added to other blocks in Minecraft, so to build something free-floating in the air the pupils will need to build a tower up to that height, which can be broken later. They may even build a city in the sky!

Class activities: Digging history

There are many ways to bring a historical element into Minecraft. The first is simple – choose a historical building that has a link to the topics you are studying in the wider curriculum. This is a common activity when using Minecraft in the classroom.

However, apart from in my own classroom, I've never seen anyone practising archaeology. There are a few ways you could do this. You or your pupils can design buildings and then bury them in the common materials you find in the environment in Minecraft. This could be time-consuming to build, so consider making a copy of the world from the previous year's class and bury their buildings for the current class to find. You can combine the historical building design with the archaeology element by asking the children to design historical buildings to play hide and seek with. Naturally, in the infinite world of Minecraft, it is important to mark out an approximate search area for your pupils; otherwise, finding a needle in a haystack would be a simple matter by comparison.

Class activities: Commanding the elements

It is possible to add modifications to Minecraft to allow you to code within the world, but this is quite tricky to set up. There is a chat function within the game that allows players to talk to each other, which I'm sure your children will make great use of. However, you can also use it to change the game in limited ways without a modification. Press the T key to open the chat function.

There is a 20-minute-long day in Minecraft. This can stifle the building activity because the builders cannot see well. You can disable the day/night cycle by typing in the chat bar:

/gamerule doDaylightCycle false

You can start it again by replacing *false* with *true*.

For a science lesson, you can change the waning of the moon by typing the following:

/time set night	[Full moon]
/time set 38000	[Waning gibbous]
/time set 62000	[Last quarter]
/time set 86000	[Waning crescent]
/time set 110000	[New moon]
/time set 134000	[Waxing crescent]
/time set 158000	[First quarter]
/time set 182000	[Waxing gibbous]

You can control many other aspects of the game, such as the weather. Type **/help** to see many more commands.

Plenary

Building in Minecraft is limited only by the imagination of your pupils and there are so many more possibilities than the few I have outlined here. Consolidate the collaboration, design and refinement skills by allowing the continual constructive feedback to flow between the children and the adults that visit this world.

Offer a final challenge to the pupils: tell them that, for reasons unknown, the staffroom will be out of action during the usual staff meeting time. Therefore, the head teacher has asked them to design in Minecraft a suitably grand, but functional, venue to hold these top-level talks.

Useful links

pi.minecraft.net Minecraft for Raspberry Pi.
bit.ly/pricomp076 Minecraft Wiki reference guide.
education.minecraft.net Minecraft in Education.
printcraft.org 3D printer for Minecraft models.

Progression

The children will cover a vast amount in Year 5. They have explored how digital mapping has changed the way we interact with the world and made it feel like a much smaller place. They have looked at how 3D computer-aided design and manufacture is changing the way industry works and how we will produce and customise our own products in the future.

Cross-curricular links

There are clear links with art, DT, history, maths and engineering. Minecraft can be used in English in many ways, with narrative story-telling being just one obvious example. Learn map skills for geography and even MFL by inviting schools from other countries to collaborate in your Realm. Science is an area where visualisation is important, and making 3D diagrams to explore would be interesting to use in class. Just imagine following sounds all the way to the inner ear, assembling molecules one blocky atom at a time, or floating though the cardiovascular system to learn about the heart!

Year 5 e-Savvy

Focus: Trolling and trails

What do I need to know?

The Web is a reflection of sociality – most people follow the rules, but just a few people can make it unpleasant for the rest of us. While misunderstandings and cross words can happen to us all, there are a few individuals that delight in being nasty and hurting others for no reason at all. It seems apt that after discussing Minecraft in the previous section, we now come to trolls.

The National Curriculum states that pupils in KS2 should:

- *Use technology safely, respectfully and responsibly; recognise acceptable/unacceptable behaviour; identify a range of ways to report concerns about content and contact.*
- *Use search technologies effectively, appreciate how results are selected and ranked, and be discerning in evaluating digital content.*

This section will address the first strand and educate the children about trolling and ways to combat it. They will also discover the extent of an individual's digital trail that they leave behind, what the dangers are and what can be done.

Interesting fact

Thousands of cyberattacks are launched every second. View the map at **map.norsecorp.com** showing just a small number of them.

Stage 1 Trolls

We have all met them – people who annoy us and are mean for no good reason. Trolling online is a very serious problem. Vulnerable people of all ages have been driven to disappear online and have been affected in the real world because of the negativity and constant insults from cowardly individuals who only want to hurt. The best defence to trolling isn't just in the technology, but also to develop a mindset and toolkit of strategies to deal with it when it occurs.

As you will see, teaching children about trolling is a delicate matter, but one that is too important not to cover in class. Because of the nature of the lesson, you should inform parents and your line manager that you will be covering this in class, detailing what the lesson will include so they are prepared and can deal with any issues the pupils might have.

You will need
- Letters to parents
- Some insults
- Thick skins
- An unkind computer via Skype or other VoIP service
- A class display with access to the Web
- A colleague with a flair for insults
- Access to the CEOP website **ceop.police.uk**

Getting started
Firstly, this lesson is as much about social skills as it is about the technology. Ensure that the pupils understand the context of the lesson and briefly explain what to expect.

Collude with another member of staff to take the role of the same rude computer we met in Year 2 (p41). This time the computer has gained a voice (provided by a member of staff via Skype audio) and the computer will begin to mildly taunt you about as many things as possible: about what you say, your appearance and the computer's low opinion of you. Agree with the insulting member of staff on a safe list of things first so they will be confident at delivering the insults well. Begin to answer back to the computer and mock a little anger. Turn to the pupils and ask for their advice. Write the best suggestions in a public space for the children to see. Talk about the differences and similarities between trolling and bullying, i.e. that one comes from someone you know, and the other is from a stranger.

Class activity: I've never been so insulted
Ask the pupils to write down their best mild generic put-downs and insults on small pieces of paper. These will range from the offensive to the plain silly. Quickly vet these and take out any that are completely inappropriate. While you are doing that, ask the pupils to tell you what they would and should do if someone said some of the things they wrote on the paper, firstly to their face and secondly online.

Online, there are a few options they could take:
- Take a screenshot of the trolling and tell an adult
- Take a screenshot and press the CEOP/'report abuse' button if available (usually located at the bottom of the website's homepage)
- Realise trolling for what it is and ignore it if it *truly* didn't bother them, although if it happens again they should use one of the first two options.

At no point should they confront a troll or reply to nasty or aggressive comments, but if they have begun to answer back they should stop as soon as they realise it is a troll. Take the pupils to a website with a CEOP button, such as **ceop.police.uk**, and show them what it looks like. Also ensure that every child is able to take a screenshot so the trolling can be evidenced if it is needed later. The method will vary with the type of device. Look for the prt scn (or similar) button on the keyboard of your PC. See take-a-screenshot.org for instructions for other devices.

Once you have finished vetting the insults, give a random set of papers to each member of the class and let them read them through quietly to get a few of the giggles out. Ask for a brave volunteer to be the victim of a public simulated trolling. Next ask that volunteer to choose someone to insult them, preferably a thick-skinned and articulate child. Before the insult comes, ask the volunteer to think carefully about how they might respond and how they might prepare themselves. At the last moment before the insult comes, stop the insulter. Ask the volunteer how they are feeling.

Send the class off into friendship group pairs to take turns at reading the insults to each other and thinking about how they would respond if the insult came from a stranger online. Keep a close eye on any of your less socially-mature and less confident pupils during this activity.

Plenary
Give the pupils an opportunity to think of all the positive things about themselves. These can be little things, such as being well-mannered, to the bigger things such as what they are good at and how they make those around them feel. Ask the class to come back together and discuss what thoughts they have had about themselves. Next, ask them to reflect on the positive qualities of their classmates and to share these. Finally, ask the children again which of the three online options (see previous page) they would be most inclined to use in response to trolling, and why.

Useful links

thinkuknow.co.uk How to have fun and stay safe on the Web.

Stage 2 The digital trail

Type your name into your search engine of choice and you will be surprised what comes up. If you have a popular name, there will probably be lots of people you don't know. But you will still be amazed to see what public information there is online about you. Search for Martin Burrett now. Go on! You will see that there used to be a firm of solicitors in Chelmsford called Budd Martin Burrett (no relation), but that many of the other results are about me. You can see photos of me and videos of me speaking at educational events. You can find all my social media accounts, educational blog posts I've written, my Flickr photostream and much more.

We all leave a digital trail which anyone can access easily. Yet many people are happy to post compromising photos of themselves to social media, add opinionated comments under online news stories, and write tweets in the heat of the moment that we then forget about. Most adults are reckless with their personal information so how are our children, who are using and posting to the Web now, before they are aware of the possible future consequences, meant to filter their content?

You will need
- Devices with access to a search engine

Getting started
Talk to the pupils about 'private' information, 'friends and family' information and 'open' information, and what level it is safe to share online (see Year 1, p11). Talk about the digital trail and that some information you post now will stay on the Web forever for anyone to look up and view, whether that is an employer or a new friend.

Ask your pupils to start their devices and go to the search engine, and then search their own name. Ask them to look at the various tabs, such as the *images* tab, and see if there is any information about them. Hopefully not.

Class activities: That's personal
Ask the pupils to search for Derek Hugglesford, a fictional person that I've added to the Web. Instruct the children to find out as much about Derek as they can and to write a profile of him. Ask the pupils to highlight information that Derek shouldn't be sharing online. Once this is collated, instruct your pupils to write an email intended to warn Derek that he is sharing too much personal information online. The email can be sent to you so you can send the email on to Derek.

Once the emails have been sent, explain that Derek isn't real. Ask the pupils to use Google Sites or Wix to create their own fictitious persona online. Remind the children not to include their own information in the profile, and that the character should live a long way from their town. Naturally, the character doesn't necessarily need to be from our time or even planet, as long as they have reliable broadband.

Plenary
Discuss the mistakes made by Derek and the pupils' own character personas. Relate this again to the levels of personal information and discuss again, because it is vital, why adding personal information to public and to private areas of the Web needs to be considered carefully.

Progression

The pupils have further developed their savviness about exposing their personal information online. They have looked at trolling and have developed strategies so they know what to do and who they can go to if they encounter one.

Cross-curricular links

There are many links with personal and social development – becoming e-savvy is as much about a mindset as the technology. There are links to creative writing and creating biographies in English, as well as links to history if the children choose a historical figure. The pupils could even add an art element by painting or drawing their character.

Year 5 Coding

Focus: 3D gaming and sensing

What do I need to know?

So far we have mainly looked at 2D games, as they are much easier to design and debug. Yet, as we've seen, 3D games like Minecraft give an immersive experience to the game play. We will begin by looking at using code to design 3D spaces. We will also look at sensing, the final area of Scratch yet to be covered, which allows sprites and the environment to interact, and for players to input information that changes the game.

The National Curriculum states that pupils in KS2 should:

- *Design, write and debug programs that accomplish specific goals, including controlling or simulating physical systems; solve problems by decomposing them into smaller parts.*
- *Use sequence, selection and repetition in programs; work with variables and various forms of input and output.*
- *Use logical reasoning to explain how some simple algorithms work and to detect and correct errors in algorithms and programs.*

Interesting fact

3D gaming is the norm today, but you might be surprised to hear that Elite, thought to be the first game with true 3D graphics, is more than 30 years old, having made its debut in 1984. (BBC Technology, 2014)

Stage 1 Kodu

Microsoft's Kodu is a 3D game design platform that is specially designed for children and education, and it is easy and fun to use. Furthermore, designing the environment of a 3D game literally takes on a whole new dimension compared to the simple backdrops that are used in 2D gaming. Kodu uses a similar idea as Scratch to link code together, but it does this pictorially with icons, rather than with blocks of code.

You will need
• Devices able to run Kodu **kodugamelab.com**

Getting started
Discuss with the pupils the pros and cons of playing and designing 3D over 2D games. Ask the children to make two lists of games they enjoy: one for 2D games and the other for 3D games. Discuss what 3D games the pupils would like to design, and note down these ideas.

Class activities: Getting around
After familiarising yourself with it, introduce Kodu to the pupils, showing them the tools at the bottom of the screen on the class whiteboard and briefly flicking through the menus.
  Once the pupils have opened Kodu on their own devices, ask them to do the following:
• Click on the *Object Tool* and place Kodu in the environment by clicking somewhere on the land.
• Right click on Kodu and select *Program* to begin to add some code to allow Kodu to move. Most code commands are separated into two parts: *When* (input) and *Do* (output).
• Ask the pupils to use the keyboard arrow keys to allow Kodu to *Move*.
• Press *Esc* on the keyboard to navigate back to the main screen and ask the pupils to click the *Play Game* button to show them that their code has worked.

Next, the pupils need to give Kodu a little more space to roam. Ask the children to use the four landscape icons, three of which look like separate squares of 3D land while the fourth looks like water, to expand the existing plot of land. Encourage them to use the *Move Camera* tool to help them see what they are doing.

Class activities: Behaviour
Ask your pupils to choose an additional sprite and work out how to code it to run away from Kodu:
When: See Kodu | Do: Move Away

Then add another sprite that shoots and changes colour when it is bumped:
When: Bumped | Do: Missile + Random

Ask the pupils to enter play mode and try to chase after the scared sprite and to see what happens when they bump into the other one. See if they can make the bumped sprite destroy the other one by making it run into it.

Next, ask the pupils to add a path to the environment and then place a new sprite at one end. Instruct the children to discover how to program the sprite to follow the path before it sees Kodu:
When: | Do: Move On Path

Add a second line of code to make the sprite attack Kodu once when they are close by:
When: See Kodu | Do: Shoot Blip Once

Finally, add some apples to the landscape and ask the pupils to discover how to make Kodu eat them:
When: Bumped + Apple | Do: Eat

Instruct the pupils to experiment to discover how to include scoring into the game, e.g.
When: Bumped + Apple | Do: Score + Red + 01 Point

Plenary
Your pupils now have all the basics they need to design a full adventure game. Ask them to build a game with obstacles, bad guys with behaviour and a points system using all the skills they have learnt.

Useful links

worlds.kodugamelab.com/browse Kodu Worlds.
welcome.projectspark.com Project Spark.

Stage 2 Sensing onscreen

As we've seen in Kodu, allowing sprites to sense each other's presence allows complex behaviours to develop. Sensing is also possible in Scratch too, and it can be divided into sprites sensing each other and their environment, but also sensing the user.

You will need
- Devices that can access Scratch **scratch.mit.edu**
- Example of an incomplete PACman game for debugging **bit.ly/pricomp077**
- Example of a platform game **bit.ly/pricomp078**
- Example of simulating gravity **bit.ly/pricomp079**

Getting started
Invite a few volunteers to come to the front of the class. Tell them to close their eyes and then give them a few objects with interesting textures to feel and identify, such as jelly, wet cornflour, cooked pasta, etc. Discuss the way in which we perceive the world and how sprites may change they behaviour once they sense their surroundings, as they saw with Kodu (see Stage 1, p113).

Class activities: Just a feeling
Tell the pupils to open Scratch and to design a backdrop with one vertical red line near the left of the screen and a blue line on the right. Ask the pupils to copy the code below into their sprite's script area, with red and blue chosen as the colours.

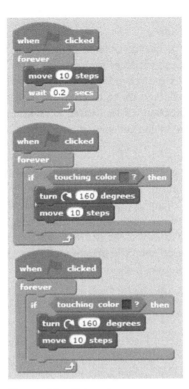

Figure 5A: Colour bounce

The pupils should adapt the code so that they have the arrow keys controlling the sprite's movements and so that touching either colour makes it 'game over'. They can stop the game using the speech blocks from *Looks* and then *Stop All* from the *Control* category.

Once the pupils have experimented and tested this, ask them to create a game with a drawn maze backdrop, where touching the maze walls results in 'game over'. A tip for drawing maze walls neatly is using the *line* tool and pressing the *shift* key to limit the angles available. Encourage the pupils to add in a few moving wall sprites that open and close passageways in the maze. Tell the children to develop the idea into a multi-level game where the sprite must get to a point in the maze where another button sprite has been placed, which is coded to change to the next backdrop for the next level.

Challenge the pupils to change the game to make it a little more forgiving by creating a 'bounce back' instead of 'game over' when they touch the walls. Ask the pupils to attempt to solve how this could be done. See the code below for one possible solution.

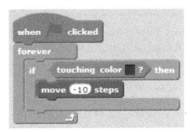

Figure 5B: Bounce back sensor

Class activities: PACing in the code

Instruct the pupils to use their 'a-mazing' skills to create a PACman game. They should draw a suitable maze, and then use variables for scores and for lives. They should add things to collect, which increases the score variable and which can disappear using the *hide* block. They will also need to include a sprite to chase your player. This will also need to obey the rules of a maze and rebound off the walls. To make the bad guy chase the player, use the *point towards* ____ block from *Motion*. See an example at **bit.ly/pricomp077**.

Class activities: Stuck in the mud

We have looked at driving games previously (see p95), but sensing can add more options to the game design. Ask the pupils to design a game where mud on the road slows the cars down. Start by instructing them to draw a race circuit with one plain colour for the off-road mud everywhere except the track. As with the driving game from Year 4 (p95), use variables to control the speed of the car. But this time, set the speed to zero for one second each time the car ventures onto the brown mud (see Figure 5C). In this way, the car will jolt a little as it makes its way back onto the track.

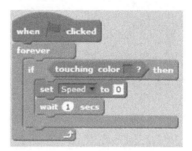

Figure 5C: Driving in mud

Class activities: Platforms

Using colour sensing is a wonderful way to create platform games. Show your pupils the example platform game at **bit.ly/pricomp078** and ask them to make something similar themselves using Scratch. Use the colour touching code to instruct the sprite that if it touches a given colour it will be repelled. Your pupils will need to add movement controls and draw a backdrop. They should also use a variable to simulate gravity (see example **bit.ly/pricomp079**).

Plenary

Ask the pupils to work in pairs to create a two-player battle game that uses sensing to detect when a player has been hit, based on the skills the children have developed over this stage and perhaps based on a theme from the wider curriculum. Examples could be an aircraft dogfight, a virtual snowball fight, or an archery game. Once they have completed their game, each pair should ask a different pair to make a copy of the game as a remix and attempt to improve and refine the game. Once complete, ask both pairs to embed their games onto the class blog for wider feedback.

Stage 3 Sensing the user

Computer games can be controlled by the players in many ways; with the keyboard, mouse and touch being just a few. Using cameras as a way for the player to use their whole body is also possible these days, and is common on gaming consoles. We will explore this idea in Scratch, as well as the technique of inputting text in order to play a game.

You will need
- Devices that can access Scratch **scratch.mit.edu**
- A copy of next week's spelling list from your English class
- Pop the balloon **bit.ly/pricomp079**
- Control the balloon **bit.ly/pricomp080**

Getting started
Start by declaring a test! Test the pupils on some spellings, maths questions and a few general knowledge questions. Ask them how gaming could make this more fun. Note the suggestions on the whiteboard.

Class activities: Coding spellings
The pupils' task is a potentially tall order – to make the weekly spelling test fun. Firstly, give the pupils their spellings for the next test. Before the pupils get started on this task, you might like to demonstrate a few useful features in Scratch to help them. Open Scratch on the class whiteboard and open a new project. Demonstrate how to make a list from the *Data* category. Show them the *ask _____ and wait* block in the *Sensing* category and the *Answer* block. Don't show them how they can use these, but encourage them to explore using these blocks in their design. Also suggest that they can use uploaded images to give a pictorial cue to the player for a particular spelling without writing the word on the screen.

   Repeat the activity with a quiz. Challenge the pupils to design a self-marking test or quiz using the *if ____ then* block with the *____ equals ____* block from *Operators* and the *Answer* block from the *Sensing* category.

Class activities: Body control
You can control many aspects of Scratch by using the webcam on your device. A very simple way to do this is to set *video motion* as a trigger, so that the proximity of movement on the make things happen, such as moving a sprite left or right on the screen. Ask the pupils to design a 'Pop the balloon' game using the *when video motion > 20* block from *Events*. See an example at **bit.ly/pricomp080**. Your pupils can also use the same trigger to change a variable, which in turn changes the motion of the sprite. See an example at **bit.ly/pricomp081**.

   Once the pupils are comfortable with the techniques, challenge them to design an exercise game for KS1. Instruct your class to conduct research into the kind of games that already exist, and which they can emulate and use as inspiration. Once they have a clear idea, they will code the project and test it out with the younger children.

   All children, and most adults, like a bit of air guitar. Using the video motion skills they have learnt to control variables, ask the pupils to design 'hands-free' musical instruments that use the video motion capability to play.

Progression

The pupils have learnt to take their skills of coding in a 2D platform to a new dimension with Kodu, including creating 3D environments, sprite behaviours and scoring systems. They have also developed their coding skills to include sensory information, both from within the game and from the player.

Cross-curricular links

Coding in a 3D environment like Kodu offers some interesting possibilities to develop orienteering and mapping skills. The sensing functions create opportunities in every area of the curriculum, but the video motion adds some interesting links to PE and dance.

Year 6 Using and understanding computing

Focus: Video, animation and changing reality

What do I need to know?

In my opinion, creating video is one of the most creative and educational tasks that children can do. It's not just crafting the shots, the research and the editing process. It is also the scriptwriting, the prop-making, the scenery design or location hunting, the costume design, the collaboration and negotiation before and during production, and the promotion, marketing and distribution of the finished product once the video has been made. Making films requires the creators to draw on many skills from the wider curriculum. In this section, your pupils will become film-makers and producers. They will learn a range of animation techniques and take video capture to new highs using drones. Finally, in this section, the children will explore expanding their digital world with a range of augmented reality and virtual reality tools.

The National Curriculum states that pupils in KS2 should:

- *Understand computer networks including the internet; how they can provide multiple services, such as the world wide web; and the opportunities they offer for communication and collaboration.*
- *Select, use and combine a variety of software (including internet services) on a range of digital devices to design and create a range of programs, systems and content that accomplish given goals, including collecting, analysing, evaluating and presenting data and information.*

This section will mainly address the second of these two strands, by showing how software and devices can be used to create video and animated content.

> ### Interesting fact
>
> The first patent for 3D film technology was by pioneering film-maker, William Friese Greene in c.1894. (Patterson, 2009)

Key words

Augmented reality (AR): The addition of sound, graphics, video or data to a user's view of the real world in order to provide a composite view.
CGI: Computer-generated imagery.

Drones: Unmanned aerial vehicles with rotor blades and usually controlled wirelessly from a mobile device or bespoke transmitter.

Onion skin: Working with more than one layer of media with sections sometimes transparent to allow the designer to see the previous image in order to help make the next one.

Chroma key: Also know as green screening. This is when software is used to replace a background of a single colour with a computer generated image, e.g. on a weather forecast map.

Storyboard: A sequence of drawings, typically with some directions and dialogue, representing the shots planned for a film or television production.

Pixilation animation: A stop-motion technique where live actors are used as frame-by-frame subjects in an animated film.

Stop-motion: Animation that is captured one frame at time with physical objects that are moved slightly between frames.

Claymation: Animation using adjustable clay figures and stop-motion photography.

Stage 1 Making movies

We live in a visual world with much of our brainpower dedicated to gathering and processing the images that hit our retinas. It is not surprising then that we find film so immersive. Anyone can record a video, but far fewer can record one well. The activities below are designed to develop film-making skills as both a technology and an art form. In this stage, your pupils will learn: to record high-quality video with sound using a range of techniques; basic video editing; to use chroma key green screen effects; to take aerial shots; and be given creative projects to try.

You will need
- Devices capable of making video and sound recording
- A range of external microphones and sound-recording devices
- Headphones
- Videos from Vimeo **bit.ly/pricomp082** (there is an album to get you started at **bit.ly/pricomp083**)
- A clapperboard (or you can clap your hands)
- An account for **dragontape.com** (share login details with pupils)
- Video-editing software
- Green Screen app by Do Ink **bit.ly/pricomp084**
- TouchCast **touchcast.com**

Getting started
Find a range of video clips with impressive shots and cinematography to show your pupils. There is a collection at **bit.ly/pricomp083** to get you started, or alternatively could use the top 10 video of films with great cinematography at **bit.ly/pricomp085**. Ask the children to comment on each film. Whilst the pupils are obviously not going to produce films with these kinds of budgets and levels of art – yet! – there is still much they can learn and emulate.

Class activities: Sound
You might think it is strange to begin this video section with activities about sound. However, it is important to address this, because with most devices you are now able to shoot a reasonable video, yet sound quality is often poor.

In advance of the lesson, record some short video clips of yourself in various locations around the school, or around the town. Ensure that you include one clip recorded in an echoey environment, and one in a small, sound-deadening location. Take the same shots with and without an external microphone.

Show these clips to the pupils and ask them to vote on which location and conditions gave the best sound quality, and how much of a difference the use of a microphone made. Ask them to think about when echo on a video is useful, for example to give a video a particular atmosphere.

Ask your pupils to scout for good locations around the school that offer a relatively quiet environment, but also the right sound quality. Tell them to make sample recordings of each location to play back using headphones.

As your film crews are probably going to be shooting one group at a time, you can invest in a wide range of equipment in small quantities and ask the pupils to experiment and choose what is right for them.

Wired clip-on microphones are relatively cheap and usually provide much better sound quality than the video device's native microphone. However, these do limit the range at which the actors can wander from the camera. Directional microphones are useful for distant shots. The best option would be to use wireless radio microphones, but these are much more expensive. However, if the sound quality is important to you, you can do as the professionals do and record the audio on a different device and each pupil can have their own clip-on microphone connected to a smartphone, small tablet or other small audio-recording device. This means the sound tracks would need to be added to the video footage in the editing process, which can cause additional problems with syncing. One way to address this is to use a clapperboard, or ask someone to clap in front of the camera when you start recording, so the images and audio can be synced. This also allows greater flexibility when adding a music track and Foley artistry (see Year 2, p33).

Class activities: Clean shots

Directors and producers spend their entire careers honing their skills to craft the best shots possible but your film crews can make just a few simple choices about how the camera will behave.

Most of the following techniques will need to be practised through exploratory play and experimentation. The pupils can do this most effectively with a few human subjects to simulate a true film set. However, many of the following techniques can be explored in miniature and en-masse in the classroom using toys, dolls and even play dough actors. The results will still be more dramatic than some actors you see!

- Technique 1: the camera should only move if you want it to – the pupils should experiment with all of the following, as each has its place in film production: using static cameras on table tops or tripods; static panning shots using tripods; moving cameras using gimbals. The worst place for a video camera is in the hand, as it will shake about. Having said this, encourage the pupils to explore tools that address this, such as Microsoft's Hyperlapse (**bit.ly/pricomp086**) – there are a range of stabilisation filters on cameras and post-production tools to help, too.
- Technique 2: shooting at different angles – the pupils should try shooting at different angles, not just at eye level, and experimenting with rotating the screen slightly to change the audience's perspective.

- Technique 3: zooming – this is a tricky thing to get right, and someone new to filming tends to overuse the zoom function because they get a bit bored when filming long clips. Instead, they should try cutting, changing the camera position and resuming. Explain to the pupils that in most films and television shows you will see, the camera shot changes position often as there are usually multiple cameras. This even happens in News programmes when the newsreader is just sitting in one position. As viewers, we are so used to this that we do not notice it. Zooming is used, but not often. Show the pupils a few clips from children's TV and ask them to see the repositioning in action to copy and practise.
- Technique 4: stopping and resuming – ideally, your pupils should use multiple devices of the same type to shoot a scene from different angles to then put together in the editing process, but they can get a similar effect by stopping the filming and repositioning their single camera, but ensuring the actors and props stay in the same approximate positions to give the illusion of continuity. Once again, ask your film crew to experiment with these possibilities and reframe from recording to just one continuous static video.

Class activities: Documentary

Because, of course, many of your pupils will be famous in the future, it is only right to document their early years by making a documentary about their school. This is a good first challenge, as it requires no additional scenery, locations or props. Ask the pupils to plan their short film carefully. They will need to storyboard each section, writing and/or drawing what they wish to include. The pupils will need to research what they might expect to be going on around the school during the day and time slot allocated for filming, and then write a draft script and any questions they might want to ask any interviewees. Once they know what they want to include, they should visit each location with the camera at a similar time of day as the real shoot will take place, to think about where they will position and move the camera and any sound equipment. If you are planning to eventually publish the video online, the pupils will need to liaise with the class teacher so they know if there are any individuals who cannot be filmed. Shots of the school outside the classroom will be relatively simple.

On filming day, the pupils will need to arrive early in each location to set up. They need to record lots of footage as short clips and move the camera, whilst trying to maintain continuity. To some extent they will be guided by what happens in the classroom as to the shots they will get. They should conduct any interviews and shoot any other atmospheric footage they need from around the school.

To minimise disruption to the running of the school, you may wish to ask just one group to film individual classes. However, if every group has shot multiple classes, you may wish to make all the footage available to all the pupils on a central server.

Class activities: Editing

Firstly, the pupils will need some practice trimming video and connecting it together. Provide your pupils with a login for **dragontape.com**. Either give the pupils a selection of vetted YouTube links for them to remix, or give them some direction about a topic to search for their own material. Ask the pupils to edit down the video to a one-minute summary of the topic. Once complete, they can embed the video to their blog. Find the 'embed' button, which looks like < / > and copy and paste the code into the blog.

Once the pupils are confident with the video-editing process, they should begin thinking about their own documentary. First of all, the pupils should sort their documentary footage into sections they wish and don't wish to use. They should put any files that they are not planning to use into one folder out of the way. However, nothing should be deleted at this point, as something might be useful later. Next, encourage your pupils to match the footage to their original storyboard to make sure they have all the clips they need.

There are many different platforms for editing videos, including iMovie, Windows Movie Maker, **youtube.com/editor** and **wevideo.com**, and you can view many more at **bit.ly/pricomp087**. Each has its unique features, but their basic functions are similar.

The pupils should drag or add the video files into the timeline in the correct order. At this stage the pupils will also need to add the audio track if they recorded it separately. They should crop the clips as they did on the DragonTape site and, for each section, the pupils will need to look carefully at the timing of the change to the next portion. They should also consider how they might use transitions, although these are seldom used in movies and on television, except the notable transition swipes seen in the *Star Wars* films.

The pupils can also add a title sequence and end credits if they wish, and then add any remaining music and soundtrack to the film. Publish the movie files, but be sure that the pupils save all the files needed to make it. The pupils should 'premiere' their film to a small group who can offer feedback, which the crew can act on if they choose.

Class activities: Chroma key

Chroma key, also know as green screening, makes it easy for your actors to appear in exotic locations. It's possible to add this effect in Windows Movie Maker (see the guide at **bit.ly/pricomp088**), but there are some applications that make this much more simple, such as the Do Ink iPad app (**bit.ly/pricomp084**) and the superb TouchCast video suite **touchcast.com**. Find an appropriately green wall, green tent or cubical walls or put up a green sheet smoothly against the wall. Avoid folds, as this will cause shadows that may appear on the final video. It is also important to get the lighting right: you will need a well-lit area and possibly additional lights to face the actors.

Next, ask the pupils to record their footage, remembering all the techniques discussed previously – it is easy to revert back to filming a single long video, rather than changing the angles of shots. The pupils need to ensure that the green continues to completely fill the background throughout and for every different shot. Depending on which chroma key software is being used, the pupils may need to add the background image for each change of angle, or you may be able to do this in one go after filming. The pupils can then edit and add to the other footage if needed.

Class activities: Films from the heavens

As a teacher, it's exciting to experiment and innovate with genuinely groundbreaking technology, and pioneer the use of technology that hasn't been widely adopted into classrooms yet. At the time of writing, using drone technology is one such area.

Drones are unmanned aerial vehicles, which usually have two or more rotors, are similar to a helicopter, and usually have an in-built camera. Some drones cost thousands of pounds, but luckily for educators the small basic models are less than £100 and the prices are dropping. They also sometimes come in kit form, so there are possible links to the Science, Technology, Engineering and Mathematics (STEM) areas of the curriculum if the children build and modify the drone. The camera offers a great opportunity to film in places and from angles that were impossible, even for professional film crews, just a few years ago. At the time of writing the UK Civil Aviation Authority requires no special licence or permission to fly drones in most places, but this is changing in many countries and you should check this is still the case when you plan to use one.

It is best if you teach the pupils how to use a drone in small groups of two or three at a time in a large open space. Taking off and landing are the hardest aspects of flying drones, so you may wish to let the pupils take control only once it is in the air. Many drones have a certain level of automation or assistance, so use it if you can. Ask the pupils to practise horizontal movements in a defined area. The children should collaborate to hone in on a stationary subject to film with the camera at a safe distance. Increase the difficulty by asking the pupils to track a moving subject. Once the children have shown some level of skill at horizontal piloting, they can move on to changing heights while filming, and also landing it if you wish. Once the footage has been transferred to a suitable device for editing, the pupils can edit and incorporate the footage as above.

Class activities: Micro opera battles

So far we have looked at using video like a big film studio, but the Web is awash with micro videos, which are only a few seconds long. Apps like Vine (**vine.co**) only allow videos of up to 6.2 seconds in length, which is restrictive, but has meant that users have had to be wonderfully creative to do things within that time.

Choose a micro video tool, such as Vine, to use. In pairs, ask your pupils to write a soap opera pilot episode to fit into the micro video's time limit. If you are using your usual video camera which doesn't have a time limit, I suggest you impose a limit of no more than 20 seconds. Instruct the pupils to prepare any scenery, props, costumes and equipment they need to make the video, then film it in the app, or record, edit and upload if necessary.

Embed the pupils' videos onto the class blog and ask the community to vote for their favourite videos. When the results are in, drop half of the shows. Show business is tough! Ask those pupils who are now without a show to team up with the pairs whose show was not axed, making a production team of four.

Brief the teams that they have been commissioned to create a further four episodes and that each team member will take a leadership role for one of them. The storyline from the first episode must continue and develop through each of the four mini shows. If you wish, you can keep the competitive element and ask the community to vote after each new round of shows. The pupils will repeat the process from the first show and publish the new episodes to the class blog.

Class activities: Television channel

Divide the class into two or three equal teams and tell them that they are going to set up some TV channels that will broadcast simultaneously in two or three classrooms (if a single form entry school; multiply accordingly if more than one form) for 30 minutes during a wet lunchtime in a few weeks' time. The rest of the school will be allowed free movement between the classrooms and the challenge will be to draw the biggest crowd at an undisclosed moment within the 30 minutes. The pupils must create a number of television shows, each under ten minutes' duration, to show during the 30-minute slot. In addition to this, the pupils need to create advertisements for fictional products to play between every show.

Tip: when I have conducted this project in my own class, I have given the pupils a phoney currency with which to make inter-team working possible. For example, if a team wishes to hire a pupil from another group, they will have to pay that group some money. The same is true for resources beyond those that the children have at their own desks, so, for example, they would pay to use paint and cardboard, etc. They also had to pay the teacher a consultancy fee if they had an unnecessary question. It is amazing how quickly they become self-sufficient! Once the video is finished, the pupils can use their remaining funds to promote their creations ahead of the showings.

The pupils' first task will be to appoint a creative director and begin to organise themselves. They will need to conduct market research into the types of shows the viewers may be interested in. After this they follow the production procedure as in previous activities, with the final 30-minute compilation of programmes and adverts being made into one long video. They will then spend some time working on promotion for their shows.

Class activities: Epic in a day

As Year 6 pupils, your class have the responsibility to lead the school in many different ways. The epic in a day movie is a great way to put all of the pupils' filming and leadership skills to the test to create something truly amazing. The idea is based on the Star Wars Uncut project (**starwarsuncut.com**), where thousands of *Star Wars* fans acted out the original film frame by frame for 15 seconds each. Some clips are very low quality, while others are amazing, but together the effect is stunning.

Divide your Year 6 pupils into pairs and ask each pair to work with a mixed-age group from the other classes to create a 15-second clip, so that every child in the school who is able to be filmed will be part of the project, which will take place on just one day. The length of the final movie depends on the size of your school; I've made a 35-minute movie in this way in just a day.

Before any filming begins, a script, costumes, props, locations and scenes all need to be ready so that only the filming and editing happens on the day itself. The script should be written by a teacher, with input from the pupils, showing what each film crew and acting troupe need to do during each 15-second clip.

The filming day will need to have regimented timing, with a realistic timetable slot for each group. Separate the Year 6 pairs into morning and afternoon groups, so one group of children are filming with younger children, while other Year 6 pupils begin editing the clips. They will swap filming and editing roles at lunchtime, so that filming and editing is happening in parallel for most of the day. Encourage the children to film in only a few shots and to delete any outtakes so they do not provide extra work to review. To use the time effectively, there should be many film crews working in different locations at the same time.

Use remote access to your school server, or cloud storage, such as **dropbox.com** or Google Drive, to send all the video files to a central storage space if possible, so the pupils do not need to worry about wires or a bottleneck of everyone needing to offload their files at once. Naturally, such a military operation will require extra support, so draft in adults from the community, or possibly contact your nearest school or college with a film and media department to dispatch students and expertise.

Once the clips have been edited, the full-length movie can be easily stitched together by a few pupils. Schedule a showing in the next morning's assembly to add greater impetus to complete it on schedule.

Plenary

Ask the pupils to compare the filming results from their first experimental filming efforts to what they have achieved at the end. Discuss what they feel they still need to improve and how they might go about it. Ask your pupils which projects they would want to do next if the time and budget was available. Challenge the pupils to take control of the filming of the next play or school production, and design promotional material to encourage the community to watch it.

Stage 2 Animation

Animation covers a myriad of different things and there are so many different ways to do it, from drawing characters to making 3D computer-generated imagery (CGI) films. Naturally, animation and filming have many similarities and the opportunity for creativity is the same.

You will need
- 'The 5 types of animation' video **bit.ly/pricomp089**
- Parapara animator **bit.ly/pricomp090**
- ABCYa! Animate **abcya.com/animate.htm**
- Lapse it app **lapseit.com**
- Devices able to access PowerPoint or other presentation programs
- Scanner
- Devices able to access video-editing software
- Cameras
- Green Blob's Adventure **bit.ly/pricomp091**

Getting started
Begin by asking the pupils to think of the different types of animation and cartoons they have encountered. Make a list of these on the board. Ask the pupils to discuss in small groups about how they think each of these is made. Watch the video about different forms of animation at **bit.ly/pricomp089**. Ask the pupils to make a simple flipbook animation, around 20 pages long, using a stack of sticky-notes. Staple the pages on the sticky section to avoid them becoming separated. Ask the pupils to share and demonstrate their flipbooks, possibly using a visualiser.

Class activities: Stop kids
Divide the class into small groups and give each a camera. Ask each group to create a simple stop motion pixilation animation with a photo camera using images of only the people and the objects around them. Show these two examples: **bit.ly/pricomp092** and **bit.ly/pricomp093**. Notice that in both examples the camera moves when it shouldn't (the background wobbles), and tell the class that they need to try to limit this by keeping the camera on a flat surface or tripod as much as possible. Once the children have collected all the images they will need, import the images into a video editor. They need to consider the frame rate of the animation to make it appear to run at the right speed. This is the number of images that appear in sequence per second. Professional films and animation have a frame rate of 25-40 frames per second, and any fewer than 10 may not produce a smooth animation. They can adjust the timing settings for how long each image remains on the screen to alter this.

Class activities: Drawing cartoons
As with the children's flipbooks in the Getting Started activity, drawing layers of slightly different drawings will create a moving image if viewed at speed. Instruct the class to go to either the Parapara animator (**bit.ly/pricomp090**) or the ABC Ya Animate (**abcya.com/animate.htm**) to animate simple cartoons. Firstly, allow them time to experiment with the tools and how onion skinning works to allow them to see the previous drawing.

Once the pupils are confident using the site, play a game of 'Animation Pictionary'. Pupils are divided into pairs. One of each pair is shown a card and they have to draw a picture to convey the word on the card to their partner. You can choose to play this activity competitively if you wish, with the first pairing to correctly guess the word on the card being declared the winners.

Divide the class into pairs and ask each pair to design a short story or instructional sequence on a topic they are studying in the wider curriculum. This could be a story narrative or perhaps an animated science diagram. Once complete, ask the pupils to watch each other's animations and then publish them on the class blog.

Class activities: Stop-motion

There are so many ways to do stop-motion. Show this example **bit.ly/pricomp094** as a demonstration of some of the things that can be done with time lapse and creative zooming. Give the pupils devices with the Lapse It app (**lapseit.com**) downloaded. Ask the children to set up their devices in busy locations and record for ten minutes. At the end of that time, the pupils will review the video and then make adjustments, e.g. in the positioning of their device, for a second, improved attempt.

Next, the pupils will try to make stop-motion claymation videos. This is a type of animation that involves using moveable clay or plasticine models to capture images frame-by-frame, moving the model a small amount each time. The children can use the automation possibilities of the Lapse It app, or they can choose to use a photo camera. and animate the images using a video editor afterwards. Firstly, watch the example, *Green Blob's Adventure*, at **bit.ly/pricomp091**, noting that the camera position changes a number of times. The pupils will need to design a set, develop a real storyline and make malleable plasticine models to make a one-minute-long animation. Once the pupils get started, suggest they practise a short sequence, such as up to their first camera position change only, in order to review what they have captured before proceeding too far – in case tweaks and improvements need to be made. Stress the importance of keeping the camera still while taking the images. Once complete, tell the pupils to add a title sequence and add it to the class blog.

Class activities: Flat-mation

Animating with paper and other materials can create some interesting effects and there are a variety of ways to do this. One method is to use a scanner in a similar way to the activities in Year 1 (p4).

- Ask the pupils to attach a background of some kind to the lid facing the scanner plate using Blu-Tack™.
- Next, ask them to cut out a few paper characters to appear in the foreground. They should affix the characters to the background using Blu-Tack™.
- Scan the image, then carefully lift the scanner lid and move the main character/s to one side, ensuring that they are once again firmly attached to the background.
- Repeat the process making sure that the characters continue in the right direction.
- Once the sequence is complete, your pupils can use a video editor to animate it.

A similar effect can be achieved using presentation software like Microsoft PowerPoint™ by adding a background and characters in the foreground, copying the whole slide, making adjustments and then repeating. You can make similar animations in the same way using **wideo.co**.

Plenary

Ask the pupils to make an animation tutorial designed for younger pupils, which is made completely with animation. Encourage the children to use a variety of different animation methods and to think carefully which order to present the different types of animation in, and how best to example the techniques to children who haven't encountered them before.

Stage 3 Different reality

The way we perceive the world is changing and we are increasingly seeing the world through the prism of a screen or website. This is taken to an extreme with augmented reality (AR), which adds a layer of graphics, data, video or sound onto the user's view of the physical real world. Google Glass is a notable example in which virtual reality aims to temporarily replace normal reality altogether.

You will need
- AR example: Earth and moon **bit.ly/pricomp095**
- Aurasma accounts **aurasma.com**
- AR example: Biology: Organs **bit.ly/pricomp096**
- AR-media SketchUp plug-in **bit.ly/pricomp097**
- Screen recorder **bit.ly/pricomp098**
- Google Cardboard **google.co.uk/get/cardboard**
- Cardboard Camera app **bit.ly/pricomp099**

Getting started
Before the lesson, print the symbol from **bit.ly/pricomp095** and set up the camera and engage the video display link (scroll down to step 2 on the website). Show the children this and explain that this is called augmented reality and it is when a computer puts a digital image over something in the real world. Provide the children with printed out markers for the resource at **bit.ly/pricomp096**, and ask them to try it for themselves on their own devices.

Class activities: Auras
Augmented Reality can be created in many ways. One great tool is Aurasma. This is a website and an app, which allows users to add images, videos and much more to a chosen image trigger which will act as a marker. Provide the pupils with login details and ask them to open the site or app, then find the *create* section. Instruct your pupils to think of a suitable marker. This could be a piece of work they have created, or a piece of artwork they have made. Add the content to be displayed and the trigger marker via upload or the device's camera.

   Once the pupils have the idea, tell them to create an augmented reality treasure hunt around the classroom or in a defined area around the school. This tool could also be used to enhance your geocaching activities (see Year 5, p98).

   For the next parents' evening, or in an area that parents and visitors access regularly within the school grounds, create an augmented display featuring triggers, such as pieces of illustrated writing, and ask the children to create a video or audio file of them reading the text or an animation giving more details. There will need to be an explanation included about how users can access the app.

Class activities: Building reality
A common use of augmented reality is to design and display 3D models so that they can be easily moved, turned and viewed by the user by manipulating the marker. In Year 5, the pupils learned to model in 3D using SketchUp (p101). Inglobe Technologies have developed

a free SketchUp plug-in (**bit.ly/pricomp097**) that allows users to take their SketchUp designs and make them into augmented reality models.

Working in pairs, ask the pupils to design a SketchUp model or find a suitable pre-designed object from the SketchUp warehouse and display it on the screen. Make sure that there is enough light to provide the necessary contrast. They should design any background scenery that needs to appear behind the computer-generated model, for example reusing the stage from their claymation filming. Tell them to use the at **bit.ly/pricomp098** to record a video of the model moving across the image.

Encourage the pupils to try the same thing again, but have actors in the background interacting with the unseen virtual object in the foreground. They can then use this technique to add objects into their other film-making projects without needing to build them. Examples may include car chases, being chased by a velociraptor, or animating aliens on top of the live action. For good results, ensure the marker and the projection size are right so that the marker cannot be seen.

Class activities: Virtual reality

The renaissance of virtual reality is gathering steam after its genesis and fall from favour in the 1990s. At that time, the technology wasn't ready to match the ambition. Now many of the biggest brands in technology are developing their own virtual reality systems. They now incorporate haptic feedback – giving a sense of touch – and adaptive audio – responding to the wearer's movements. Virtual reality is poised to give users a truly immersive experience.

Until this technology can transport your class to different locations and the wild places of the world, you can introduce virtual reality in your classroom using Google Cardboard. The tech giant has developed a system that allows users to use a smartphone in the place of a virtual reality headset. You can either order an inexpensive cardboard frame from **google.co.uk/get/cardboard** or you can ask the pupils to download and make their own following the instructions at **bit.ly/pricomp100**. There are now a growing number of compatible apps available for Google Cardboard at **bit.ly/pricomp101**.

Ask the pupils to use the Cardboard app and maps to visit a number of famous places and take a look around. Ask the pupils to design a soundscape (see Year 2, p32) to provide a most immersive experience of the sights they are viewing.

Ask the pupils to use the app 'Cardboard Camera' at **bit.ly/pricomp099** to create a virtual reality 3D surround-image tour of the school and the wider community. The app works in a similar way to an ordinary photo camera, but multiple images will be taken and then stitched together by the app. Follow the on-screen tutorial for details. Next, instruct them to build a 360-degree miniature scene that uses elements of the wider curriculum. This could be the inside of a hill fort, a Victorian street scene, or an imagined scene from a book or from their creative writing.

Plenary

Ask the pupils to bring together animation and the virtual reality experience by making a zoetrope virtual surround photo – a spinning cylindrical device used in Victorian times to give the illusion of a repeated moving animated image. Choose one pupil to be the photographer. Mark a central point on the floor with chalk for the photographer to stand on and then draw a circle a good radial distance from the central mark. Choose another pupil to stand in the outer circle. The photographer takes a series of photos of the individual, who should change position between each shot. The photographer will need to signal when it is safe for the person to move. The idea is that you are recreating a zoetrope, in which the same person is shown in different poses as the viewer turns. If time allows, try quickly changing costumes using the same technique. For example, this could be used to show different clothes through time.

Useful links

bit.ly/pricomp102 Spacecraft 3D – NASA AR App.
bit.ly/pricomp103 Google Cardboard Design Lab app.

Progression

The pupils have gained the skills to move from recording a quick video to producing and organising, editing and publishing high-quality films. They have explored various types of animation and learnt how to use most of them with digital technology. The pupils have also begun to discover the possibilities offered to them by augmented and virtual reality to transport them to other places and times, and to add additional information to the world around them.

Cross-curricular links

Video, animation and virtual reality have so many different applications within the wider curriculum. Explanation becomes easy when using the moving image. Drama and storytelling in English are obvious examples, but recording and replaying video to improve sports technique, time lapsing art projects from beginning to end, and depicting historical scenes are all possible with video and animation.

Year 6 e-Savvy

What do I need to know?

Being in Year 6 isn't easy. Pupils are in the twilight period between childhood and teenage responsibility, and it is our duty to ensure they are ready and independent before the night falls. Being organised is the first step to being independent. We will begin by looking at how technology can be used to plan, track tasks and work in sync with those around us. Then the pupils will learn how to fend for themselves against the biggest threats in the digital world: malware and viruses.

The National Curriculum states that pupils in KS2 should:

- *Use technology safely, respectfully and responsibly; recognise acceptable/unacceptable behaviour; identify a range of ways to report concerns about content and contact.*
- *Use search technologies effectively, appreciate how results are selected and ranked, and be discerning in evaluating digital content.*

This section will focus on the first strand by helping pupils be responsible in both their on- and offline pursuits, and by learning about the dangers of malware and steps to avoid it.

> ### Interesting fact
>
> In 1981, the first large-scale computer virus was written by Richard Skrenta and was called Elk Cloner; however, the idea of the computer virus can be traced back to 1949, when John von Neumann's article on the 'Theory of self-producing automata' was edited and completed by Arthur W. Burks, and published by University of Illinois Press, in 1966.

Key words

Crowdsource: Getting help or resources from a large number of people via the digital medium.

Stage 1 Being organised

Do you find yourself reminding your pupils about the same thing again and again? My advice is to push the responsibility onto the children – and technology can help.

You will need
- A fairly long video about a topic from the wider curriculum
- Devices that can access
  - Google Keep **keep.google.com**
  - Google Calendar **calendar.google.com**
  - The do it yourself notepad **ifttt.com/products/do/note**

Getting started
Part of being a teacher is breaking information and skills down into challenging but manageable pieces. Forget all that for a moment.

Tell the pupils that they are going to write a story and then very quickly read off something like the following criteria:
- The story must take place by the sea, but no boats are to be mentioned
- The main character must have a pet, but not a dog, cat, hamster or tiger
- The pet speaks, but only in precisely seven-word-long sentences
- The main character has a magical backpack containing a tent, a kayak, a thimble, a sewing kit, a rug, washing-up gloves, a shovel and dog biscuits – all of these must be mentioned in the story! The backpack cannot contain a map, a torch, any digital technology or food.

This list is designed to confuse and panic. Ask the pupils if they are clear on all of the criteria. Hopefully, they won't be. Discuss how they could remember all of the criteria and prompt them towards the answer – making lists.

Class activity: Digital lists
For the example above, a handwritten list would be sufficient, but there are many digital tools that can make list-making much easier. My favourite is a small but powerful list-maker from Google (**google.com/keep**) and I like it for three reasons:
1. It's everywhere – you can access it from smartphone apps, the website and even a Chrome browser app
2. It's collaborative – you can share the notes with any Google account holder
3. It is multimedial – you can text, draw, use your voice or take photos as notes.

Show your pupils a fairly long video about a topic from the wider curriculum and instruct them to write notes using Google Keep. At the end of the video, ask some pupils to read out some of their notes, but ensure that the others do not add to their lists. Ask the pupils to share their lists with you via Google so you can show them on the whiteboard and 'crowdsource' (work as a class to improve) the notes. Ask the pupils to pick out ideas which others noted but they did not. Ask them to tally how many extra pieces of information they can see in one particular pupil's notes compared to their own.

Assign one pupil per table as a scribe for every lesson – they must record instructions digitally for others to refer to as a public note. As there will be many scribes in the room, there is a good chance that most points will be added to the single collaborative document written together by the scribes. Then, if anyone asks for information that has already been given, you can refer them to the notes. Pupils can add any important dates, such as homework and tests, to a shared Google Calendar **calendar.google.com**. You could also introduce the do it yourself note **https://ifttt.com/products/do/note** to help pupils do this in just few clicks.

Plenary
At the end of every day the pupils can copy and paste the notes into a post on the class blog to provide a pre-eminent and searchable reference. Ask the pupils to use blog comments to feedback to the note-takers about what they found useful and what needs improvement in future.

Useful links

droptask.com Make visual and intuitive lists.
evernote.com Save projects, ideas and lists.

Stage 2 Digital threats

Getting a computer virus or other malware can cause lots of heartache. Not only can it stop the normal function of your device and stop your access to your important files, but malware can also get your private information, passwords and financial information into the hands of criminals. As the pupils venture out into the digital world alone, they need to be prewarned to be pre-armed.

You will need
- BBC video and guide, 'What are viruses and malware?' **bit.ly/pricomp104**
- Devices with accessible anti-virus software

Getting started
Ask the pupils what they think a computer virus is and what it does. Record their answers on the whiteboard without confirming the answers. Ask if they have heard of malware and note down any suggestions too. Show the two BBC videos at **bit.ly/pricomp104** and talk through the rest of the information. Ensure the pupils realise that malware comes in many forms, and at best will slow down your device, and at worst will make your device unusable and steal your information for criminals. Furthermore, no digital device, even a mobile phone, is immune to attack.

Class activity: Thinking and scanning
The weakest link in digital security is often the users themselves. Malware can be added to a computer in many ways. Take suggestions for possible infection routes from the pupils and note them down. A few leading routes are:
- Visiting an infected website
- Clicking on a link that downloads malware

- Downloading programs from unsafe locations
- Via emails and spam
- Clicking on banner advertisements
- Connecting to the wrong open Wi-Fi network.

Reiterate that thinking and being cautious is the first step to staying safe. The other main step is ensuring that your device has adequate and up-to-date anti-virus software. Ask your pupils to run a virus scan on a device. Note that this may not be possible on networked computers and may need the help of your network manager, or you might be able to bring in an old device from home.

Discuss the fact that when you download an app from either of the two biggest app stores you are presented with a list of the permissions and access that app has to your device. Most people just agree, but ask your pupils to look carefully at these permissions for some examples and whether it is justified. For example, does a clock and alert app need access to change your files, access to your address book, and access to your browser history?

Plenary

Digital threats are real and they are a fact of life, but we can do a lot to prevent them happening. Ask the pupils to make an information video, infographic (see p80), animation or podcast highlighting the damages and prevention methods necessary to stay safe from malware, aimed either at the staff, parents or their fellow pupils.

Progression

The pupils have learnt about ways to stay organised in their studies and work collaboratively – these skills and tools are transferrable to their life outside of school. The class have also looked at how to prevent malware compromising their devices.

Cross-curricular links

Planning, collaborating and being organised are beneficial in all subject areas, but may be particularly useful in subjects such as English and science, where they are essential to the process.

Year 6 Coding

Focus: Coding animation, apps and final fun

What do I need to know?

Your pupils will now be proficient coders, and in this section they will apply their ideas within programs. 3D animation using coding will be a new challenge, but one built on the coding knowledge they have acquired over the previous five years. App building will again offer new challenges and new opportunities, but will be familiar to the children from the website-building skills they developed in Year 4 (p78). The final stage will be the culmination of all their coding know-how, employing the skills they have learnt within a grand project.

The National Curriculum states that pupils in KS2 should:

- *Design, write and debug programs that accomplish specific goals, including controlling or simulating physical systems; solve problems by decomposing them into smaller parts.*
- *Use sequence, selection and repetition in programs; work with variables and various forms of input and output.*
- *Use logical reasoning to explain how some simple algorithms work and to detect and correct errors in algorithms and programs.*

Each of these strands will be covered in this section, with a particular focus on the decomposing of ideas to develop their designs in 3D animation and game design.

> ### Interesting fact
>
> At its launch in July 2008, Apple's App Store only had 552 apps. (apps-world.net, 2013) Compare that to 1.5 million as of June 2015! (statista.com, 2016)

Stage 1 Coding animation

You may have noticed that 3D animation was not covered in the previous animation section. We shall now rectify this by looking at how an animator can use code to create and make their sprites act out a scene.

You will need
- Devices able to access Scratch **scratch.mit.edu**
- Devices able to access Looking Glass **lookingglass.wustl.edu**

Getting started
Ask the pupils to code the following in Scratch: two sprites walk on stage, meet, have a short dialogue and then walk off the stage. Review the short animations – you may wish to record some using a screen recorder, for example Apowersoft **bit.ly/pricomp098**.

Class activity: Coding 3D animation
Scratch is good at animation, but Looking Glass is even better. Instruct the pupils to open the platform – they will need some login details – and work through the following set of instructions, which will take them on a brief tour of the program to explain where the main features are, and enable them to become familiar with it. There is an example that I have produced for you to use as a demonstration with the pupils, if you wish, entitled 'Frozen World', which can be found at **bit.ly/pricomp105**.
- The pupils should choose a blank canvas and click *Edit Scene* in the corner of the stage.
- Next, they should browse the collection of sprites and choose two in the first instance, plus one prop. In 'Frozen World' I have chosen to use Thor, a panda and a castle gate as a prop, but ask the pupils to make their own choice.
- Drag each sprite and the camera to their starting positions and edit their characteristics using the panel on the right.
- Once they are happy, ask them to click *Edit Actions* from the corner of the stage. The pupils will now see a screen that is not dissimilar to Scratch. They can switch between sprites. In *Thor's Actions* area in 'Frozen World', there are different categories for the things I can code Thor to do.
- Ask the pupils to follow these instructions to make one of their sprites speak. I want my sprite, Thor, to say 'I am Thor'.
  - I drag the *Thor say Text* block from the *say, think* category.
  - As the block is dragged, the option to change the text will appear. Click *Custom Text* and change the value.
  - A *More* drop-down menu will appear at the end of the block with many formatting options. Find *duration* and set for two seconds.
- I also want Thor to turn towards the panda while he is saying this. Scroll down the *Block bank* window until you see the *Action Ordering Boxes*. Drag *Do together* into the *My Story* area.
- Now drop the previous *'I am Thor'* block into the *Do together* block.
- Find and create *Thor turn to face panda duration 4.0 seconds* and add it to the *Do together* block.
- Click *Play & Explore* near the top of the screen to view what the code does so far.
- From the menu under the stage, choose *camera*. Add this to the *Do together* block: *camera move towards Thor 2.0 meters duration 4.0*.

- Review using *Play and explore* and tweak the code to improve the camera position.
- On the same block, change *Thor* to *Thor head*, so the camera zooms in to Thor's face.
- From the menu under the stage find *panda* and then *panda head*. Ask the pupils to use the *Panda head turn to face Thor* block.
- After that, tell the pupils to get the panda to say 'Hello Thor' for a few seconds.
- Then tell the pupils to make the prop do something, such as making the castle gates open.
- Then tell them to discover how to make the sprites turn and walk off.

There are many more examples of short animations for you to explore on the Looking Glass platform itself.

Now that the pupils have the basic idea, ask them to work in pairs to storyboard a short sequence on paper first, and then to design the scene on the Looking Glass animator. The storyboard might be to ask them to reimagine a scene from a book or their own writing, to re-enact great moments of history or to use the animator to code MFL dialogue.

Ask the pupils to view each other's animations and to remix one group's efforts if they think that they can add something more.

Plenary

Create an epic using short clips of animation from each group as outlined in the filming section of this chapter (p126). Agree on a storyline and assign a section of the story to each group. Once complete, use the *Share As* option or use a screen recorder to capture the animation and stitch together using a video editor.

Useful links

alice.org Alice 3D animator.
blender.org Blender animator.

Stage 2 App design

App, short for application, is now a general term used to describe a self-contained piece of software (which is most software), but it has become synonymous with mobile phones and app stores. In this stage, the pupils will build a basic browser app designed for a mobile phone. Designing apps for an app store is quite tricky to do, so this is just an introduction to the possibilities at a basic level using mobile browser apps instead.

You will need
- An account with AppShed **appshed.com** or alternative
- Devices able to access AppShed

Getting started
Begin by defining what an app is, and discussing with the pupils about their favourite apps and what makes a good one.

Class activities: Making it 'app'en
Provide the pupils with login details for AppShed or your alternative. The free *Starter* account should be sufficient for your uses. Choose the AppBuilder, fill in the details for registration and then click *New App*.

Ask the pupils to build an app for the school. They should start by changing the screen name. Then, using the *Standard Screen Items*, ask the pupils to add some images, text and a link to the school's website. From the *Advanced Screen Items*, they should add a *Map Point* to show the location of the school. Next, tell your pupils to go to a new tab and create a gallery of generic photos of the school. After this, the pupils can continue to customise the app.

Once the apps are complete and checked to ensure no personal information or sensitive images have been included, they can be published and viewable on a mobile device. Ask the pupils to work in groups of five or six to look at each child's app in turn and to offer feedback and improvements.

Class activities: Topic app
The subject matter for an app is limitless. Ask the pupils to design revision apps for the rest of the class based on various upcoming topics, skills, ideas and content they will meet during the next term. Assign each pupil a different topic and team the children in subject-specific groups (a science group, a maths group, etc.) so they can have some support from their peers. Even though each topic and lesson will come up at a different time, the pupils should have the same deadline for completion to keep it fair. When their particular lesson arrives, that pupil should be allowed to give a short presentation about the app and about the topic to begin the learning for the others.

Plenary
Each pupil should keep the school app they designed above (see Making it 'app'en) up-to-date with new information and improvements for a month, or a length of time of your choosing. They will need to take newsletters and other information from the main school website, as well as publishing their own news articles on the app. Suggest that each pupil shares the web address for their school app with their parents.

Stage 3 Producing games, not just code

There is more to producing games and other programs than the game play. In this section, the pupils will learn about how to package games with a suitable title screen, storylines, instructions and levels.

You will need
- Devices able to access Scratch
- A brief history of video games **bit.ly/pricomp106**
- Devices able to access dragontape **dragontape.com**
- Mario Bros.™ game openings **bit.ly/pricomp107**

Getting started
Begin by discussing the early evolution of gaming. Watch the video at **bit.ly/pricomp106** and ask the pupils to pay particular attention to the information on storylines in gaming. The video stops with gaming in the 1980s. Ask the pupils to create their own videos to continue the story to the present day using YouTube clips and **dragontape.com**.

Class activity: Titles, levels and plots
The pupils are going to use all of their coding knowledge and skills to design multi-level Scratch games with title screens, in-game instructions and a plot for an 'Open Arcade' event that Year 6 will hold for the rest of the school, where they get to play the games your class have created.

At the outset, make it clear how much class time will be given to this project so they are able to plan. Ask the pupils to watch either the opening sequence of Super Mario Bros. 2™ on **bit.ly/pricomp108** or Yoshi's Island **bit.ly/pricomp109** for an easy example of how to include a story.

The first step is to plan. Divide the class into groups of four or five to discuss ideas for games that can work over a number of levels. Encourage them to be bold, but realistic. They should research online for possible ideas, but use the simplicity of the ideas shown in the early evolution of gaming video above (**bit.ly/pricomp106**) as a guide.

Ask each group to outline their idea on paper and then make a *'Dragon's Den'*-style presentation pitch of their idea to the rest of the class, who will offer feedback and pick holes in their idea to encourage improvement. You (or the pupils themselves) may wish to assign specific tasks to individuals within the group.

Once the idea has been well thought out, the pupils can begin designing their individual games. They should begin the design by adding a title screen using a backdrop, and sprite buttons to navigate to other pages. If the game has a 'game over' it should return to this title screen automatically. Encourage the pupils to use the show and hide functions to ensure the right sprites appear on the various screens. The children can choose to add simple instructions to the title page, or whether to include a separate backdrop.

From the title screen, the pupils should include some storyline element. This could be in the form of a series of simple static backdrops that change automatically or require a key press to continue – they can also consider rolling text or audio input. The pupils must indicate when a new level is reached, perhaps with a 'next level' title screen or with the level permanently displayed in a corner. A new level is a chance to extend the storyline further. If the game has a 'game over', the pupils will need to signal when this happens and return to the title screen.

Plenary
Once the games are complete, the pupils should invite a small number of beta testers from their class and from other classes to try out the game to find bugs, provide feedback and offer suggestions for improvements. After these have been made, the children are then ready for the 'Open Arcade' event. Once the event is over, the pupils can publish their games to the class blog.

Progression

Over the three stages the pupils have learnt how to use code to animate in 3D environments and manipulate 3D props and sprites, and have learnt the very basics of computer-generated animation. The children have been introduced to the basics of app building and they have brought together all their coding skills into one final large-scale project that has moved their individual one-screen games into a multi-levelled blockbuster.

Cross-curricular links

As we've seen, 3D animation coding can have many links to other curriculum areas, such as English, drama, maths and even science and PE, as the designer moves the different sections and limbs of the body. Apps are just as flexible as the website the children built in Year 4 (p78), and the subject matter is limitless.

Bibliography

apps-world.net (2013), 'Five flabbergasting facts and figures as the App Store turns five'.
   (https://apps-world.net/2013/07/11/five-flabbergasting-facts-and-figures-as-the-app-store-turns-five/)

BBC Technology (2014), 'Elite: the 'first 3D video game' redeveloped'. BBC News
   (www.bbc.co.uk/news/technology-30576913)

BBC Technology (2015), 'Spam email levels at 12-year low'. BBC News
   (www.bbc.co.uk/news/technology-33564016)

Burrett, M. (2015), 'Making the difference'. UKEd Magazine
   (http://ukedchat.com/2015/12/02/ukedmag-making-the-difference-by-ictmagic/)

Cbbc newsround (2014), 'Guide: what is bitcoin and how does bitcoin work?'
   (www.bbc.co.uk/newsround/25622442)

Clark, R. N. (2005), 'Notes on the resolution and other details of the human eye' (clarkvision.com)
   (www.clarkvision.com/articles/eye-resolution.html)

DfE (2013), National Curriculum in England: Computing Programmes of Study. Crown copyright

Krotoski, A. (2010), 'Robin Dunbar: we can only ever have 150 friends at most'. The Guardian newspaper
   (www.theguardian.com/technology/2010/mar/14/my-bright-idea-robin-dunbar)

Lafrance, A. (2015), 'How many websites are there?' The Atlantic
   (www.theatlantic.com/technology/archive/2015/09/how-many-websites-are-there/408151)

McMillan, R. (2015), 'Her code got humans on the moon – and invented software itself'. Wired.com
   (http://www.wired.com/2015/10/margaret-hamilton-nasa-apollo)

Patterson, J. (2009), 'A history of 3D cinema: from the 19th century to James Cameron's 'Avatar' –
   everything you want to know about 3D films'. The Guardian
   (www.theguardian.com/film/2009/aug/20/3d-film-history)

statista.com (2016), 'Number of available apps in the Apple App Store from July 2008 to June 2015'.
   (www.statista.com/statistics/263795/number-of-available-apps-in-the-apple-app-store/)

Wallop, H. (2009), 'Video games now bigger than film'. The Telegraph
   (www.telegraph.co.uk/technology/video-games/6852383/Video-games-bigger-than-film.html)

Ward, M. (2014), 'How to make money finding bugs in software'. BBC News
   (www.bbc.co.uk/news/technology-25258620)

Use of material

Screenshots of Scratch have been used in accordance with point five of MIT's Scratch policy **scratch.mit.edu/terms_of_use** under a Creative Commons Attribution-ShareAlike 2.0 license. Scratch is developed by the Lifelong Kindergarten Group at the MIT Media Lab. See **scratch.mit.edu**.

Audacity screenshot obtained at **http://audacityteam.org/about/images/audacity-windows.png** and modified in accordance with **http://audacityteam.org/copyright**. The audacityteam.org site is licensed under a Creative Commons Attribution License, version 3.0.

Images of Sonic Pi have been used in accordance with the policies outlined at **https://github.com/samaaron/sonic-pi/blob/master/LICENSE.md**

All links to UKEdChat sites, related documents and resources are the author's own material.

Every reasonable effort has been made to trace copyright holders of material reproduced in this book, but if any have been inadvertently overlooked the publishers would be glad to hear from them.